WITHDRAWN

From Toronto Public Library

The Mohawk

Titles in the Indigenous Peoples of North America Series Include:

The Apache

The Blackfeet

The Cherokee

The Cheyenne

The Comanche

The Hopi

The Inuit

The Iroquois

Native Americans of California

Native Americans of the Great Lakes

Native Americans of the Northeast

Native Americans of the Northwest Coast

Native Americans of the Northwest Plateau

Native Americans of the Plains

Native Americans of the Southeast

Native Americans of the Southwest

The Navajo

The Pawnee

Primary Sources

The Sioux

The Mohawk

Mary R. Dunn

LUCENT
BOOKS ®

THOMSON
GALE

San Diego • Detroit • New York • San Francisco • Cleveland • New Haven, Conn. • Waterville, Maine • London • Munich

For more information, contact
Lucent Books
27500 Drake Rd.
Farmington Hills, MI 48331-3535
Or you can visit our Internet site at http://www.gale.com

LIBRARY OF CONGRESS CATALOGING-IN-PUBLICATION DATA

Dunn, Mary R.
    The Mohawk / by Mary R. Dunn.
       p. cm. — (Indigenous peoples of North America)
Includes bibliographical references and index.
Summary: Discusses the origins, ceremonies, festivals, and leadership of the Mohawk people of New York, as well as their relationship with the European settlers.
    ISBN 1-59018-005-4 (alk. paper)
    1. Mohawk Indians—History—Juvenile literature. 2. Mohawk Indians—Government relations—Juvenile literature. [1. Mohawk Indians. 2. Indians of North America—Michigan.] I. Title. II. Series.
    E99 .M8 D86 2003
    974.700'9755—dc21

                                  2002010429

Printed in the United States of America

Contents

Foreword   6

Introduction
The Mohawk   8

Chapter One
The Place of Flint   10

Chapter Two
People of the Place of Flint   22

Chapter Three
The Friends and Enemies of the Mohawk   33

Chapter Four
Ceremonies and Rituals   46

Chapter Five
Lost Lands and New Lifestyles   57

Chapter Six
The Mohawk in the Twenty-First Century   69

Notes   81
For Further Reading   84
Works Consulted   85
Index   89
Picture Credits   95
About the Author   96

Foreword

North America's native peoples are often relegated to history—viewed primarily as remnants of another era—or cast in the stereotypical images long found in popular entertainment and even literature. Efforts to characterize Native Americans typically result in idealized portrayals of spiritualists communing with nature or bigoted descriptions of savages incapable of living in civilized society. Lost in these unfortunate images is the rich variety of customs, beliefs, and values that comprised—and still comprise—many of North America's native populations.

The *Indigenous Peoples of North America* series strives to present a complex, realistic picture of the many and varied Native American cultures. Each book in the series offers historical perspectives as well as a view of contemporary life of individual tribes and tribes that share a common region. The series examines traditional family life, spirituality, interaction with other native and nonnative peoples, warfare, and the ways the environment shaped the lives and cultures of North America's indigenous populations. Each book ends with a discussion of life today for the Native Americans of a given region or tribe.

In any discussion of the Native American experience, there are bound to be similarities. All tribes share a past filled with unceasing white expansion and resistance that led to more than four hundred years of conflict. One U.S. administration after another pursued this goal and fought Indians who attempted to defend their homelands and ways of life. Although no war was ever formally declared, the U.S. policy of conquest precluded any chance of white and Native American peoples living together peacefully. Between 1780 and 1890, Americans killed hundreds of thousands of Indians and wiped out whole tribes.

The Indians lost the fight for their land and ways of life, though not for lack of bravery, skill, or a sense of purpose. They simply could not contend with the overwhelming numbers of whites arriving from Europe or the superior weapons they brought with them. Lack of unity also contributed to the defeat of the Native Americans. For most, tribal identity was more important than racial identity. This loyalty left the Indians at a distinct disadvantage. Whites had a strong racial identity and they fought alongside each other even when there was disagreement because they shared a racial destiny.

Although all Native Americans share this tragic history they have many distinct differences. For example, some tribes and individuals sought to cooperate almost immediately with the U.S. government while others steadfastly resisted the white presence. Life before the arrival of white settlers also varied. The nomads of the Plains developed altogether different lifestyles and customs from the fishermen of the Northwest coast.

Contemporary life is no different in this regard. Many Native Americans—forced onto reservations by the American government—struggle with poverty, poor health, and inferior schooling. But others have regained a sense of pride in themselves and their heritage, enabling them to search out new routes to self-sufficiency and prosperity.

The *Indigenous Peoples of North America* series attempts to capture the differences as well as similarities that make up the experiences of North America's native populations—both past and present. Fully documented primary and secondary source quotations enliven the text. Sidebars highlight events, personalities, and traditions. Bibliographies provide readers with ideas for further research. In all, each book in this dynamic series provides students with a wealth of information as well as launching points for further research.

The Mohawk

Centuries ago when Native Americans moved along the Susquehanna River and set up their longhouse villages around Lake Ontario and along the Mohawk River, they found a land rich with forests, wildlife, lakes, and streams. It was the perfect setting for communal living.

Since there are no written records of the first Native American settlements, historians rely on the oral history of the tribes for dates, events, and traditions. The Iroquois settlements probably occurred in several different migrations. Clusters of people likely came together or broke off from other groups because of a common dialect or tradition. Around A.D. 900, the ancestors of the Kanien'kehake, or "People of the Flint," settled in what is now the eastern part of the state of New York. The Algonquian Nation called them "Mohawk."

The Mohawk are part of the Iroquois Nation, a confederacy of tribes that flourished in the late fifteenth and early sixteenth centuries, and still exist today as a distinct group of people committed to their language, culture, and fundamental sense of community. Many historians believe that the framers of the U.S. Constitution were influenced by the Iroquois system of government, in which the people chose representatives to make decisions for the good of all.

The original confederacy consisted of five tribes, or nations: the Mohawk, Seneca, Onondaga, Oneida, and Cayuga. Later a sixth nation, the Tuscarora, joined the group. The Mohawk were the easternmost tribe of the Iroquois; their territory extended from the Delaware River north to the St. Lawrence River and included almost all of the Adirondack Mountains. To the east were Lake Champlain, Lake George, and the Hudson River. It was here that the Mohawk set up their longhouse communities and became the "Keeper of the Eastern Door."

In the early years, the Mohawk people had their land to themselves. The tribe grew, spread, and prospered. Men built longhouses, hunted, and fished. The women planted crops, cared for the children, and cooked for the members of the longhouse. Small villages of longhouses cropped up in many locations along the Mohawk River Valley.

When Europeans began to arrive in the New World, the resources that had drawn the Mohawk to the area also attracted settlers. Many French and Dutch colonists saw the advantages of living in the rich territory and trading their wares of household goods, tools, and glass beads with the Mohawk for beaver pelts. The European products enriched the lives of the Mohawk, but also brought the problems of learning a new culture. Sometimes against their will, the Mohawk were drawn into conflicts between two opposing groups. On other occasions, the warriors of the tribe fought aggressively to defend what was theirs. The vigor with which they clashed with their enemies made the Mohawk feared by their rivals. Through all of their conflicts to retain land and their independence, the Mohawk maintained their rich cultural life, including participating in ceremonies and practicing rituals that had their roots in the spirit world.

Even though the Mohawk eventually lost much of their land, and the governments of Canada and the United States tried to change Iroquois cultural practices, the Mohawk have endured as a part of the Iroquois Confederacy. Today, the Akwesasne reservation in New York State is home to approximately seven thousand Mohawk people. Other Mohawk choose to live away from the reservations or make their homes on reserves in Canada. No matter where they dwell, the symbolic longhouse remains as an institution, and the Iroquois sense of community lives on in the Mohawk traditions of the twenty-first century.

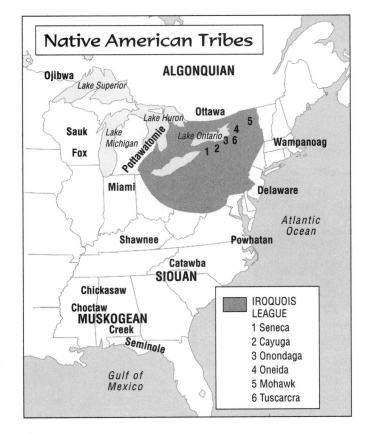

Chapter 1

The Place of Flint

The history of the Mohawk Indian tribe is older than the story of the United States. It began long before the recorded history of the country. The Mohawk tribe is one of the five founding nations of the Iroquois Confederacy. The members of this closely related group of Native Americans are the Mohawk, Oneida, Onondaga, Cayuga, and Seneca. Modern historians have dated the origins of the Iroquoians to the period between A.D. 900 and 1450. They settled in an area that is now largely in the state of New York and occupied approximately thirty-nine thousand square miles.

The Mohawk lands lay between the Delaware and the St. Lawrence Rivers and included almost the entire Adirondack Mountain range, bordered on the east by Lake Champlain, Lake George, and the Hudson River, and reaching north to the St. Lawrence. Within this spacious territory, the geography and climate of the Mohawk River Valley helped shape the culture of the Iroquois Nation.

A Good and Fruitful Land

In 1644, Johannes Megapolensis, a Dutchman traveling through the Mohawk River Valley, described the environment of this rich land:

The land is good, and fruitful in everything, which supplies human needs. The country is very mountainous, partly soil, partly rocks, and with elevations so exceeding[ly] high that they appear to almost touch the clouds. There on grow the finest fir trees the eye ever saw. . . . In the forests is [a] great plenty of deer. There are also many partridges, heath-hens and pigeons that fly together in [the] thousands, and a great number of all kinds of fowl, swans, geese, [and] ducks which sport upon the river in thousands. Beside the deer and elks, there are panthers, bears, wolves, and foxes. In the river is a great plenty of all kinds of fish—pike, eels, perch lampreys, cat fish, sun fish, shad, bass, and sturgeon.[1]

As Megapolensis observed, the Iroquois had at their disposal many natural resources. The woodlands provided trees for building their dwellings and gave them firewood. Flatland areas near the rivers could be used for farming. Forests housed wildlife for hunting or trapping. The rivers and lakes supplied fish as well as a means of travel by canoe. The land was also rich in minerals: iron, garnet, talc, gypsum, and flint. Because of the abundance of flint in the land of the Mohawk, they were given the name "People of the Place of Flint."

Not only were the resources plentiful, but the climate of the Northeast provided lush vegetation and was suitable for farming. A Roman Catholic priest of the Jesuit order, François-Joseph le Mercier, who traveled through the Mohawk River Valley in 1656, compared the territory to his homeland: "The climate there is temperate, the seasons succeeding regularly as in France while the soil, in various parts, is adapted to the growth of all the products of Touraine and Provence."[2]

The temperatures were hot during the summer, yielding about 120 frost-free days, and rainfall was plentiful for a growing cycle. In the winter, however, cold temperatures forced the Mohawk to create warm shelters. Unlike many Native American peoples who lived in tepees or wigwams,

The Mohawk River today. The river took its name from the native people who farmed, fished, and hunted in its environs for centuries before the Europeans arrived.

A typical Mohawk longhouse. Covered with the bark of trees, each loaf-shaped longhouse was home to several families from the same clan.

the Mohawk had rectangular, communal homes known as longhouses that were shared by several families belonging to the same clan. As a result, the Mohawk were also known as Haudenosaunee, or "People of the Longhouse."

Locating and Constructing Longhouses

The location of the longhouse was as important as the resources of the land that surrounded it. The Mohawk concept of the division of earth and space—originating in the creation myth passed down through the generations that explained how the sky existed first, followed by water, and finally land—favored a clearing surrounded by

forest. The tribe preferred to build their longhouse villages on an elevated stretch of land surrounded by a palisade, a row of long pointed stakes forming a fence for fortification. Another important component of the longhouse site was its nearness to arteries of transportation, the lakes, streams, and rivers.

The journal of Harmen van den Bogaert, a Dutch surgeon who traveled through the Mohawk River region with the help of Indian guides in 1634 and 1635, gives a firsthand account of a longhouse village. From a European perspective, he refers to the longhouse settlement as a "castle" situated on an elevated stretch of land above the Mohawk River:

In the morning we went together to the castle over the ice that had frozen in the waterway during the night. When we had gone one half mile, we came into their first castle that stood on a high hill. There were only 36 houses, row on row in the manner of streets, so that we easily could pass through. These houses are constructed and covered with the bark of trees, and are mostly flat above. Some 100, 90, or 80 steps long; 22 or 23 feet high.[3]

As a guest in the village, van den Bogaert was able to observe closely the workmanship and construction materials used in building the longhouses. In his journal, he recorded,

Poles made from saplings, several inches in diameter, were set in the ground following a generally rectangular floor plan. The tops of these poles were drawn together and secured, forming vertical or near-vertical walls and an arched or arbor like roofing 15 to 20 feet high. Once this framework was erected, it was covered with sheets of elm bark, leaving an entrance, usually one at each end. Movable bark sheets at the apex of the roof could be adjusted to provide for light and ventilation.[4]

Archaeology Offers Keys to the Past

Archaeologists who studied the Mohawk River Valley where villages were built at various time periods discovered a great deal about the habits and history of the people who lived there. One area of study was the longhouse. The findings at one site dated back to 1350 and revealed the outline of a dwelling that probably housed four families. In another location of the same time period, they found dwellings that held twice as many families. After 1400, archaeologists think that the Iroquois probably separated into tribal groups and the size of longhouses, as well as the number of longhouses in a village, increased. The general pattern of development over time seems to support this. By 1630, the typical longhouse was probably large enough to accommodate fifty people. In addition to the longhouse itself, archaeologists studied artifacts found near the longhouses. These artifacts sometimes revealed information about patterns of movement. Inhabitants of a longhouse village relocated for different reasons. For example, residents of one longhouse village might migrate north in the summer to escape the heat and relocate farther south for the winter to avoid extreme cold. Farming needs were another reason the tribes moved. Inhabitants of larger villages tended to relocate, perhaps as often as every decade or two, when they recognized that crops were becoming inferior in quality and the land was becoming fallow because of overplanting. When this occurred, the longhouse community moved on to a new area with richer soil.

One site that yielded valuable archaeological information about the Mohawk lifestyle was the village at Garoga. It is the best-known Mohawk village site (1525–1580), located on a hilltop in the town of Ephratah, New York, about seven miles from the Mohawk River. Archaeologists found the remnants of nine longhouses there. Like other Mohawk longhouses, they were about twenty feet in width but differed in length from about 125 to 226 feet long. For fortification, the men built a double palisade to surround the southwest access. Samples of subsistence remains that were found include corn, beans, hickory nuts, hazelnuts, and acorns. Bones of human fingers were also discovered at the site, which may be attributed to the well-documented torture practice of amputating fingers.

The rich data supplied by archaeologists provides valuable information about the living areas and movements of a people. Archaeological findings can also help to explain the rise and fall in population.

Population Trends

Between the years 900 and 1634, archaeologists suggest that one cause of the increased numbers of Mohawk and other Iroquois tribes was the adoption of one group of Indians into the tribe of another to make up for the loss of life within the victor's tribe. Artifacts from one tribe found at the site of another support this theory. The upward population trend was reversed, however, when Europeans moving into the area brought with them diseases for which the Native Americans had no immunity. In 1634 many Mohawk died as a result of a smallpox epidemic, which spread quickly in some longhouse communities. The epidemic caused the total Mohawk population to drop by more than 50 percent. Some warriors may have escaped the disease because they traveled and may have been away from their tribe during the crucial period of the contagious illness.

In about the middle of the fifteenth century, the Mohawk had begun grouping in villages of six hundred to eight hundred people. This clan system served as a means of organizing family living.

The Clan System

The clan system was the Iroquois unit of social organization. The Mohawk Nation was divided into three clans: the Bear, the Wolf, and the Turtle. Every Mohawk belonged to one of these clans. Sometimes the image of the clan animal was displayed prominently, high on the outside of the longhouse. Some anthropologists believe that the clans were not equal in importance. They suggest that the Turtle clan claimed to be superior because of its association with the Mohawk creation myth, the people's version of the story of how the world came to be.

A clan shared a common ancestry or lineage. Because the mother was considered the head of the family, the Mohawk formed what is called a matrilineal society. Children lived with their mother, father, sisters, and brothers. This group made up the fireside family of the longhouse. The father might be with the family for a time, but often he was away from the longhouse

Creation Myth

In almost every culture, there is a story that explains how the world came to be. The Mohawk had their own version of the creation myth based on oral tradition. In Joseph Bruchac's article *"A Mohawk Village in 1491: Otstungo,"* he tells the Mohawk's creation story.

"The woman in Skyland dreamed that the great sky tree must be uprooted. She was expecting a child, and her dream was strong. So her husband, the Skyland chief, had the tree uprooted. The woman looked through the hole left by its roots and saw the earth far below—unlike the earth of today, for there was no land, only water. As she looked in wonder, she slipped. She clutched at a tree branch that lay near the hole but only stripped away a handful of seeds . . . and [she] fell. . . . The geese flew up and caught her between their wings. . . . The other birds and animals, seeing she needed a place to stand, dived down to bring up earth from the bottom [of the water] . . . . The Great Turtle offered its back as a place to spread the earth. . . . The woman . . . stepped onto this new moist earth and dropped the seeds [she was holding]. . . . From these seeds grew the first plants. And when the child was born—that child was a girl . . . who would marry the west wind."

hunting or protecting the clan.

Children inherited the clan affiliation of their mother, so they also lived with their maternal grandmother and aunts and the husbands of these relatives. This made up what was called the longhouse family or community. Thus, each Mohawk belonged to a fireside family, a longhouse community of several fireside families, a village, a clan, the Mohawk Nation, and the League of the Iroquois.

The clan matron, who was usually the oldest or most respected female member of the group, headed each clan. She was responsible for the welfare of the clan. Her job was to counsel the people of her clan and to nominate, install, and, if necessary, remove a male chief. The clan matron also named all the people in her clan.

Archaeologists at the Garoga site noted the pattern of longhouse placement in the village and considered a possible link to the concept of the clan. In *Mohawk Valley Archaeology: The Sites,* Dean Snow elaborates:

> It is tempting to infer some connection between the existence of three clans in Mohawk society and the presence of three sets of three longhouses at this site. Perhaps each of the three sets was built by lineages of the same clan. It is even possible that

this was the dominant Mohawk village at the time of the formation of the Iroquois Nation. However, all of this is merely speculative.[5]

In addition to being the foundation of the longhouse family, clans were also grouped together for different reasons to form larger divisions. The three Mohawk clans were sometimes divided into two groups called moieties. At times, the Wolf and Turtle clans formed one moiety, and the Bear clan formed the other. At other times, the Wolf and Bear clans were joined, and the Turtle clan formed a separate moiety.

Clan groupings of moieties were important in carrying out the ceremonial and political functions of the Mohawk tradition. Social gatherings were one occasion when clan members framed into two groups in order to compete in games. Another time that required the larger grouping of clan members was in times of grief.

Politically, the clan as a whole acted on behalf of individuals. If a member of one clan committed a crime against the member of another clan, the clan of the offender had to make peace with the members of the clan of the offended. Similarly, clans had

An artist's rendering of a Mohawk longhouse community. Family and political affiliation organized these communities.

Wampum

According to the Iroquois tradition, Hiawatha invented wampum from beads made of purple and white shells. However, archaeologists think that wampum existed before the Iroquois Confederacy, which Hiawatha helped to found. Wampum beads—ground, polished, and bored through the center—were strung and made into belts or straps.

The wampum belt had various uses. It decorated a chief to show his office. As a way of recording tribal history, the wampum belt's design told a memorable story. During councils, it was a symbol to remind those present that only kind and gentle words could be spoken while the wampum was displayed. In a treaty, it was used to convey negotiations. The bearer of the wampum belt represented the one-minded agreement of the Mohawk people: the men, women, children, and even future generations. To the recipient of the message, it meant the messenger brought "truth."

After the coming of European traders, beads for the wampum belt were usually made of glass and were the exchange medium given to the Indians for animal pelts. In 1899, the Iroquois at Six Nations sold eleven wampum belts to local dealers. They were later brought to the Museum of the American Indian in New York City. After much effort, the beads were finally returned to the tribe in 1988.

A Mohawk wampum belt depicts peace and friendship between the Iroquois Nation and American colonies.

to approve the adoption of new people into the group and give permission for the distribution of farmland to members.

The Dawn of the Confederacy

The smooth functioning of the clan system was successfully maintained by the rules of the Iroquois Confederacy. According to Iroquois oral history, there was a time when all the tribes of the region seemed to be in turmoil. Villages were in constant conflict, and one tribe fought another. Cannibalism was the accepted way of sealing the fate of one's enemies. In *The Iroquois,* Snow explains the motivation for this treatment: "The torturers attempted to invest themselves with the bravery and prestige of their victims. . . . Children were anointed with the blood of brave victims, and warriors consumed their hearts, so that they might acquire a portion of the victims' courage."[6]

In this dangerously unstable political environment, thoughtful leaders developed the idea for a confederation of the five Iroquois tribes. Later, the Tuscarora joined the alliance to make six tribes in the league.

Although the period of conflicts among tribes is factual, the story of the wise stranger who led the people to peace contains mythic elements. As the legend goes, Deganawida, an outsider from the region near Ontario, was overcome with sadness and horror by the bloody conflicts and violence among tribes. A holy man who became known as the Peacemaker, Deganawida had a dream in which he saw the five Iroquois nations unified, and his message after that was that they must live in harmony and justice by forming a set of laws.

The Peacemaker's Vision

Accompanied by an Onondaga brave named Hiawatha, Deganawida traveled from village to village seeking consensus among the feuding tribes. The message of Deganawida and Hiawatha was to form a union and establish laws that would bring warring tribes together.

The Iroquois Confederacy arose as a result of the Peacemaker's efforts to help create one nation that remained multinational. In *The Six Nations of New York*, an Onondaga chief of the nineteenth century explains Deganawida's mission:

The Peacemaker's vision extended to all the people of the earth then known to him. He erected a symbolic tree that has come to be called the Great Tree of peace. This tree was intended to symbolize the law and would be visible from a great distance to all nations.

The Peacemaker unified the nations of the Confederacy into one nation under an ideology that was complex but whose symbols were easy to grasp. The longhouse, which had been a dwelling in which extended families resided, became the symbol of a nation: the sky was compared to its roof; the earth was like its floor; and the fires burning inside were like the nations stretching east to west. The people of a nation hold fast to the idea of a united nation, and the Peacemaker introduced ideas to promote unity.[7]

From east to west, villages of the Iroquois spanned the area that is now central New York State like one giant longhouse. Because the Mohawk tribe was located east of the other tribes of the Iroquois Confederacy, it received the name "Keeper of the Eastern Door." The Seneca guarded the western door, and the Onondaga Nation was the keeper of the fire in the central hearth.

The unity of the five nations was illustrated in other graphic ways. One representation was of five arrows bound with

The Legend of the Peacemaker

Because the legend of the founding of the Iroquois Confederacy comes from oral tradition, there are many different versions. It has not been proven that an Indian by the name of Deganawida existed. But the founding of the league did occur, and its principles became a model for modern democratic government. The following version of the legend is from *The Iroquois* by Dean Snow.

"It was a time when war was the normal state of things. North of Lake Ontario there was a young, [pregnant] Huron woman. . . . In due course the child, a boy, was born . . . [and] named Deganawida.

Deganawida grew quickly to become a handsome young man. He had a natural gift for speaking and preached to the children of the community. His message [was] of peace through power and law. But he came up against the doubt and jealousy faced by all prophets in their own countries. . . . Announcing his intention to depart, he built a stone canoe and launched it . . . . He passed from west to east through Iroquoia, urging the hunters . . . to take his message of peace back to their chiefs.

The Peacemaker [Deganawida] moved on, stopping among the Onondagas. . . . He quickly converted Ayonhwathah [Hiawatha] from cannibalism . . . and charged him with converting . . . a particularly malevolent shaman. . . . The Peacemaker left to travel to Mohawk country. . . . They accepted his message [of peace] and became founders of the League. . . .

Meanwhile, . . . the shaman killed each of [Hiawatha's] three daughters. Devastated by grief, [Hiawatha] left the village. . . . Along the way he came to a lake. A flock of ducks flew up to allow him to pass dry shod, carrying the water with them and revealing a lake bottom strewn with shell beads. These [Hiawatha] collected in a buckskin bag. Some he strung on three strings as a symbol of his grief. . . . He eventually encountered the Peacemaker. . . . Together they sang the Peace Hymn. . . .

The Peacemaker and [Hiawatha] taught the ritual to the Mohawks . . . the Oneidas . . . the Onondagas . . . [and] the Cayuga. . . . Then with the chiefs of the four nations, they went to the Senecas, who also joined as older brothers, completing the League [of the Iroquois]."

deerskin; another was of five wampum-belts tied together. A third showed a circle of five chiefs holding hands. Their bond could not be broken, even by a falling tree. The tree image also served as a connection to the creation myth of Skyland. With these visual reminders of unity, the people had the strength of the confederacy's principles always before them.

Principles of the Iroquois Confederacy

Scholars debate the exact date of the founding of the Iroquois Confederacy, or

A Description of the Land of the Mohawk

In 1642, Johannes Megapolensis, a young clergyman, was chosen by a Dutch patron to preach to the settlers in the New Netherlands and later to the Indians. Megapolensis wrote to his friends about his experiences with the Mohawk, and these translated letters provide a great deal of information about the land and customs of the tribe. Taken from the volume edited by Dean Snow et al., *In Mohawk Country*, the following is an excerpt from one of Megapolensis's letters describing the territory.

"There are also in this country oaks, alders, beeches, elms, willows, etc. In the forests, and here and there along the water side, and on the islands, there grows an abundance of chestnuts, plums, hazel nuts, large walnuts of several sorts, and of as good a taste as in the Netherlands, but they have a somewhat harder shell. The ground on the hills is covered with bushes of bilberries or blueberries; the ground in the flat land near the rivers is covered with strawber-ries, which grow here so plentifully in the fields, that one can lie down and eat them. Grapevines also grow here naturally in great abundance along the roads, paths and creeks, and wherever you may turn you find them. I have seen whole pieces of land where vine stood by vine and grew very luxuriantly, climbing to the top of the largest and loftiest trees, and although they are not cultivated, some of the grapes are found to be as good and sweet as in Holland."

Legendary Mohawk chief Hiawatha departs on a peacemaking journey.

the League of the Iroquois, but the work attributed to Hiawatha and Deganawida probably was completed by 1525. The Iroquois Confederacy is considered by many researchers to be the oldest continuously functioning government "of the people" on earth. The underlying ideals of right-eousness and peace helped Deganawida gain support and enabled him to introduce civil authority to the tribal people.

The organizational structure of the confederacy resembled a pyramid, as described by the historian Hazel Hertzberg in *The Great Tree and the Longhouse:*

> Each village in Iroquoia [the Iroquois lands] had its own village council, which looked after village affairs. Members of the council were men—clan representatives chosen by the Clan Matron of each clan in consultation with the other women of the clan. Each village had a head chief, who presided over the village council. Thus village government consisted of men who represented clans and who were chosen by women.
>
> Although the details are not clear, it appears that each nation or tribe had a council made up of these head chiefs of the villages. The tribal council managed tribal affairs.
>
> In turn, the Confederacy Council consisted of the tribal chiefs. . . . This council of Confederacy Chiefs had jurisdiction over all the member nations in certain matters. Once elected, a Confederacy Chief held office for life, unless he was removed for a serious offense.[8]

The League of the Iroquois was a sophisticated political system in which members were governed by what today would be identified as an unwritten constitution. Their rules for choosing representatives, though complicated, suggest an appreciation of the concept of checks and balances. Although they rejected the concept of majority rule, which is often considered the principal characteristic of a democracy, the Iroquois Confederacy is often described as a democracy because of the elaborate system of representation and the willingness of authorities at each level to listen to the opinions of the spokesmen. At each ruling level, matters for discussion were probably presented by an orator who looked to the audience for approval as he spoke. Differing opinions were heard from one side and then the other, but if consensus could not be reached, the matter was dropped.

Protected by the laws of the Iroquois Confederacy, the Mohawk people within their clans and longhouse communities were influenced by the geography and climate of the Mohawk River Valley. Their surroundings helped mold them into the "People of the Place of Flint." From this combination of influences, their daily lifestyle evolved.

Chapter 2

People of the Place of Flint

The people of the Mohawk tribe built semipermanent communities in geographic areas suitable for farming, hunting, trading, obtaining building materials, and traveling on waterways. The Europeans compared these hilltop settlements to castles, constructed on a site with a view of surrounding areas to give advance warning of the approach of enemies. Because of the Northeast's seasonal changes, which bring a rhythm to daily life, spring was the time for the Mohawk to prepare the fields for the new growing season. In summer, crops had to be tended. Activities such as gathering berries and repairing the living quarters kept clan members busy. When autumn came, hunting, harvesting, and storing food for winter required the help of young and old. By the time winter descended into the valley, the people of the longhouse gathered around the fire, busying themselves with making tools and weapons and listening to stories passed down from generation to generation. So it was that within the longhouse community,

uniform housing arrangements, routine customs, and daily activities regulated the lives of the Mohawk people.

Inside the Longhouse

Inside the longhouse, the clan members had a place to sleep and a communal fire for cooking and heat. In *The Great Tree and the Longhouse,* Hazel Hertzberg provides realistic images of the arrangement and atmosphere of the interior of the longhouse:

> After the bright sunlight outside, the inside seems very dark. The longhouse smells of wood-smoke and cooking and people. As your eyes grow more accustomed to the dark interior, you see that you are in a kind of vestibule. Firewood is stacked here, and there are a number of bark barrels in which food is stored. Beyond the vestibule stretches a long corridor about 8 feet wide. Down its center a number of small bowl-shaped hearths have been scooped out of the earthen

floor. Here the women cook in the winter. One fire serves two families.[9]

Mealtime was somewhat different from the modern-day idea of cooking and eating. The women cooked once early in the day, and the family ate only one shared, full meal, usually in midmorning. In *The League of the Iroquois,* Lewis Morgan, later known as the "Father of Anthropology" and the first to write in detail of the Iroquois people, describes the usual diet: "Their principal articles of food were cracked corn, and skinned corn [hominy],

two or three varieties of corn bread, venison and other game, soups, succotash, charred and dried green corn prepared in different ways, wild fruit, ground nuts . . . resembling wild potatoes, beans and squashes."[10] Berries and plants were also part of the nutritional diet of the Mohawk family.

Johannes Megapolensis, who ate with the Mohawk while in their village, further describes their food and eating habits:

Their bread is Indian corn beaten to pieces between two stones, of which they make a cake, and bake it in the

Mohawk women grind corn and prepare food while men construct a new longhouse. Usually, two families shared a cooking fire inside the longhouse.

Women cook inside their longhouse. The Mohawk diet consisted of corn, berries, fish, game, and other foods found in the woodland environment.

ashes; their other victuals are venison, turkies, hares, bears, wild cats, their own dogs, etc. The fish they cook just as they get them out of the water without cleansing; also the entrails of deer with all their contents which they cook a little; and if the intestines are then too tough, they take one end in their mouth and the other in their hand and between hand and mouth they separate and eat them.[11]

Food was placed before the family in one large pot, and all family members gathered around it to eat. Men ate first; the women and children ate later. However, any leftover food could be eaten at other times during the day. If a visitor came to the longhouse, a dish of whatever had been prepared for the family was set before him; a wife was expected to offer this hospitality. A hot beverage, brewed like tea from the tips of the hemlock boughs, was a favorite drink.

Besides attention to diet and manner of eating, living areas within the longhouse had a prescribed form. The sleeping arrangement in the longhouse was similar to built-in benches or bunk beds. Morgan says there were "wide seats, . . .

of bark boards, about two feet from the ground, well supported underneath, and reaching the entire length of the house. Upon these they spread their mats and skins, and also their blankets, using them as seats by day and couches at night."[12]

In "A Mohawk Village in 1491: Otstungo," writer Joseph Bruchac, a Native American author and storyteller, gives other details about each individual family's compartment within the longhouse:

A blanket of skins may be drawn across the front, though the fire's warmth is preferred to privacy when the winds are cold. Beneath the elevated sleeping benches one places personal items one does not wish to share—a tool, pouch of medicine, a special clay pipe. No one, not even the smallest child will disturb them.[13]

Infants and Young Children

Within the intimate space of the longhouse, children were nurtured under the watchful care of the women of the extended matriarchal family. However, the newborn began his or her life outside of the longhouse community. Childbirth was considered a time of danger for the clan. When the mother-to-be was about to give birth, she moved to a hut set apart from the general living areas, just as she did each month during her menstrual period. With the assistance of one or two women of the clan, she stayed there until the birth.

The Snowshoe

Because of the need to travel in heavy snowfall, the Iroquois invented snowshoes for hunting and pursuing the enemy, especially in little-traveled areas like the forests. In *The League of the Iroquois*, Lewis Henry Morgan describes their construction.

"The snow shoe was about three feet in length by about sixteen inches in width. A rim of hickory bent round with an arching front, and brought to a point at the heel, constituted the frame, with [the] addition of cross pieces to determine its spread, . . .

a network of deer strings, with interstices [spaces] about an inch square. The ball of the foot was lashed at the edge of this opening with thongs, which passed around the heel for the support of the foot. The heel was left free to work up and down, and the opening was designed to allow the toe of the foot to descend below the surface of the shoe as the heel is raised in the act of walking. It is a very simple invention, but exactly adapted for its uses."

A few days after the child was born, the mother and infant returned to the longhouse community. It was there that the child remained closely supervised by the mother and the mother's female relatives. If the women needed to leave the indoors to attend to chores, the infant accompanied them, usually fastened in a cradle board. When the mother found it necessary to free herself of her burden to work, the cradle board was hung from a tree branch, where the child could watch the activities from an adult eye level. It was important to the tribe's people that children had the same point from which to view the world as their elders.

As soon as the young child was able to walk, he or she went to the fields to help with planting and harvesting, worked in the longhouse, and participated in ceremonies. But children had recreation, too. They enjoyed playing hoops and darts. Sometimes they entered into the adult games of snow-snake or lacrosse. At other times, especially during festivals, children might go from house to house asking for presents.

Spanking was never used as a form of punishment. Instead, dousing with water was the most common way of disciplining a child for unacceptable behavior. If this method of correction did not work, a relative would pretend to be Longnose, a mythical cannibal clown. Young children, frightened by the fearsome costume, usually changed their behavior as demanded.

The Burden Litter and Strap

The Mohawk people had no backpacks or motorized vehicles to help them transport items. Usually the objects had to be carried, but devices called the "burden litter" and another attachment, the "burden strap," helped them move objects from one place to another more easily. Depending on the type of load to be moved, the burden litter could be carried on the back. Lewis Morgan describes them in *The League of the Iroquois*.

"[The burden litter was a] necessary appendage to every house, to the traveller and to the hunter. Sometimes they were elaborately carved and finished, but more frequently were of a plain piece of hickory. . . . The frame consisted of two bows of hickory, brought together at right angles, and fastened to each other by means of an eye and head. The upright part of the frame is the same as the horizontal in all particulars except its great length. Strips from the inner rind of basswood bark were then passed between the bows both length and crosswise, and fastened to the rim pieces. A burden strap was attached to the frame."

Older Children

At the age of eight or nine, life changed for Mohawk children. From their mother, maternal grandmother, and aunts, the young girls learned to cook and sew. Preparing food for storage or eating took a great deal of time. Crops had to be harvested and dried. Roots, nuts, and berries had to be gathered and stored in bins in the longhouse so that there would be enough food within easy reach when winter came. Sewing was another time-consuming task that was the responsibility of women. Making clothes for the family involved preparing animal hides, cutting the skins, and decorating the garment with beads or quills.

Mohawk boys spent time in the fields and forest. Through the summer, they camped where new crops were planted to drive any animals away that might eat the young plants. The boys also joined the men to learn the skill of hunting or trapping. Since there were no schools, the education of the young, which consisted of learning the ways of the tribe, was provided by adults in the longhouse community. As the children matured into adults, they took on new roles themselves.

Young Adults and Marriage

When it was time to enter the adult world, adolescents, boys and girls alike, went to the forest alone to fast, meditate, and receive a guardian spirit. Sometimes they reported having visions. After that experience, they returned to the longhouse to take on the duties of adults. The boys took on the responsibility of helping the men to hunt, trap, fish, and defend the longhouse village. The girls assisted with additional chores around the longhouse.

The time for young adults to marry was decided on by the older members of each clan. For the most part, the mothers decided the choice of a partner. When a mother thought her son was suitable for marriage, she looked for a maiden who would be compatible with his temperament and personality. When she found one, she negotiated the marriage with the mother of the bride. The young people were not consulted.

After the adults had decided on the match, the maiden was taken by her mother to the house of her future husband. The girl carried a few cakes of unleavened corn bread, which she presented to her future mother-in-law as a way of showing her domestic skill. The young warrior returned a gift of venison to the mother of the bride to show that he would be able to provide for his household. This exchange of presents bound the new pair together as man and wife.

The marriage commitment was sacred, but if a couple wanted to end their relationship, they could receive the approval of an elder woman and be given permission to separate.

The Role of Women

The social, domestic, and political life of the village revolved around the self-reliant, able-bodied women of the Mohawk tribe.

Socially, the women's clan was the dominant family unit. When men married, they lived with the family of the wife and their children became members of her clan. The women of the tribe usually had no more than three children. By limiting the number of dependents through the use of herbal potions that induced miscarriages, so-called abortion medicines, the women of the clan made sure that they would be strong enough to carry out their daily duties and that there would be enough food for everyone in the longhouse community.

Within the longhouse community, the females of the tribe maintained the rhythm of domestic life because the men were often away. Food production from planting to harvesting was the responsibility of the women, and they followed a prescribed ritual. As soon as the leaves on the oak trees were as large as a squirrel's ear, the women knew it was time to plant. Bruchac describes the women's ceremony of preparing the corn for planting: "Only the fattest and best-shaped kernels taken from the center of the ears have been soaking the past several days in herbal tea that only the women know how to mix, potions that soften the kernels and keep away crows and insects. Only the women are entrusted with the corn, for plants are female and thus responsive to the powers of women."[14] Squash and beans were planted later. The three crops—corn, beans, and squash—were the special gift of the Great Spirit and were associated together as the "Three Sisters." At harvest time, the community worked together to dry the corn, beans, and squash and stored them in elm

bark containers to supply food for the longhouse during the cold months ahead.

Another domestic chore was the making of clothing and household items for members of the clan. Women prepared hides, sewed, and decorated garments. In *The Great Tree and the Longhouse*, Hertzberg gives some details of the process: "Buckskin tanned with deer brains was fashioned into skirts for the women, leggings and breechcloths for the men, and moccasins for both. Clothing and moccasins were decorated with fine moose hair and porcupine-quill embroidery."[15] Sometimes their clothing was also decorated with beads arranged in colorful, symbolic patterns. The care the women took to prepare outer garments for the family provides some idea of the Indians' attention to personal appearance.

The idea of adorning the body also included other details. Megapolensis, the Dutch clergyman who wrote letters home about his travels among the Mohawk, gives his impression of the tribe:

> The people and Indians here are like us Dutchmen in body and stature; some of them have well formed features, bodies and limbs; they all have black hair and eyes, but their skin is yellow. . . . They likewise paint their faces red, blue, etc, and they look like the Devil himself. They smear their heads with bear's grease, which they all carry with them for this purpose in a small basket. They say they do it to make their hair grow better and to prevent their having lice.[16]

Lacrosse

Lacrosse is a sport played by many young people today. However, Native Americans have enjoyed the game for centuries. The Mohawk people believe the creator gave them the sport. The following excerpt from Hickok Sports' "Sports History: Lacrosse" (www.hickoksports.com) explains how the game got its name.

"Among Native Americans there were many versions of what we call lacrosse. . . . The Six Tribes of the Iroquois, in what is now southern Ontario and upstate New York, called their version of the game 'baggataway' or 'tewaraathon.'. . . According to most accounts, the first Europeans to see baggataway played were French explorers who thought the stick the players used resembled a bishop's crozier—la crosse, in French—so the sport was given a new name. However, the French played a form of field hockey that was called jeu de la crosse, and that's a much more likely origin of the name."

Mohawks enjoy a game of baggataway. The Mohawk played the game for centuries before the arrival of the French, who renamed it "la crosse."

Politically, the Mohawk women enjoyed a degree of influence unusual among Native Americans. It was up to the women of the village to advise the clan matron in the choice of the males who would represent them. The selected men became sachems, or chiefs, at the Great Council to make laws and settle issues. Elders among the women also served as counselors to the tribe.

The Role of Men

The Mohawk men were hunters, fishermen, traders, and warriors, as well as governors. Leaving their longhouse villages, the Mohawk found well-stocked hunting grounds near the Delaware and Susquehanna Rivers and north near Lake Champlain. They hunted deer, elk, moose, bear, and beaver. The bow and arrow was the most common weapon, but they also used traps, spears, and nets to catch prey, including birds and fish. The Indian had a great respect for the gifts of nature and did not waste them. In "Otstungo," Bruchac tells of the harmony that the Mohawk believed exists between the human and animal world: "We are like our brothers, the wolves. . . . We hunt the deer, but we do not wipe them out. If there are too many, they will starve. If we hunt them in the fight way, the Deer People will be stronger and their children's children will survive to support our own children to come."[17]

Keen observers of nature, the Mohawk hunters were very knowledgeable about wildlife. They knew that deer returned to the same paths almost daily, and they used this information to track and ultimately capture their prey. Similarly, an Indian hunter knew the size and weight of an animal he was tracking by the depth and size of its tracks in the snow. The hunter had to be prepared to use strategy to outsmart his prey so that the animal would not pick up on the human scent. Just as the deer could sense the presence of the hunter, the hunter also had sensitivity toward the animal. As he took aim to kill his prey, the Mohawk said a prayer of thanks to the animal, as he was taught to use the gift of life well.

Besides their jobs as hunters and fishermen, the men of the Mohawk tribe were also traders. Because the Mohawk men traveled from place to place, both individually and in groups, they encountered other tribes, as well as European immigrants. Evidence of Onondaga chert in Iroquois sites far from the source of this flintlike rock alerted archaeologists of the possible trade of materials. Similarly, European artifacts were found at many longhouse sites. Because transporting merchandise was an important part of trading, the canoe served as the vehicle of choice. Their canoes, made of red elm or birch bark, ranged from twenty-five to forty feet in length. For trade purposes, the Mohawk coasted the lakes and rivers carrying as much as twelve hundred pounds of fur pelts. When the men were not engaged in hunting, trading, or other activities, they helped to create objects for use in the longhouse.

Arts and Crafts

Although the Mohawk men and women made items to assist them in their everyday life, they also created beautiful art objects in the tradition of their ancestors. Basket weaving was a craft at which the Mohawk excelled. The art of basketry began with the work of gathering and preparing the materials. Men cut sections of bark from ash trees. The women prepared them by cutting them into thin strips and soaking them until they were pliable. Then they were woven with sweet grass to make an attractive container. Large baskets were sometimes used for storing food; the smaller baskets held household items or functioned as a piece of artwork to commemorate a special event.

Pottery was another craft that demonstrated the artistic talents of the Mohawk people. Like basketry, pottery making was both an expression of art and the creation of a useful container. In *The League of the Iroquois*, Morgan tells of the artisans' advanced techniques: "Some of these specimens of black pottery, which is the

A Mohawk pot dated from A.D. 1500. The banded collar at the neck of the pot is a distinguishing feature of Mohawk pottery.

best variety, are of so fine a texture as to admit of a tolerable polish, and so firm as to have the appearance of stone."[18]

Archaeologists who studied the remains of pottery at various sites in New York can trace the development of the craft and the migration of the people using the objects by examining the shards found at certain digs. At one settlement, Owasco, archaeologists reported, "The pots were more elongated and more globular than later vessels. Collars [bandlike rims on pots] were rare at first, but became more common later on."[19] Archaeologists also found pipes made of clay. Sometimes the bowl of the pipe was shaped into a human face or given the form of an animal. Interestingly, pipes were often found at great distances from the longhouse community, which further shows that men traveled from the community and were seldom limited to the confines of the longhouse.

Outside Influences

Although tradition prescribed roles for the Mohawk men and women within the longhouse community, the tribe did not exist in isolation. One Iroquois longhouse community often needed to communicate with another, and neighboring tribes interacted with each other. As the Europeans settled nearby, this presented not only opportunity for trade but also unknown dangers. With these outside influences ever present, the Mohawk people found themselves surrounded by friends and enemies.

Chapter 3

The Friends and Enemies of the Mohawk

Accounts of people's efforts to live peacefully with one another are as old as the story of man. The Mohawk were loyal friends but formidable foes.

After the voyages of Christopher Columbus, other explorers from Europe became interested in North America. At first, most of them traveled only along the Atlantic coast. However, in the seventeenth century, French and Dutch explorers ventured inland and established settlements. The Europeans brought with them prosperity and new products that enriched the lives of the Mohawk; however, they also changed the life of the tribe in many ways. These early explorers, traders, and missionaries provided the first written accounts of life in the Mohawk villages. Many of them formed close friendships with members of the tribe.

Tribal Friends

In the fall of 1609, Henry Hudson, an Englishman employed by the Dutch to find a passage to the Pacific Ocean, came to the Mohawk River Valley. Although he failed in his primary task, he did eventually set up a trading post near Albany, New York. In explaining events recorded by Harmen van den Bogaert, twentieth-century editors Charles Gehring and William Starna note the importance of Henry Hudson's discovery of the resources of the New World:

> The natural resources that drew these merchants to the coast of America were the beaver. Current fashion in Europe required a steady flow of pelts for the hat-making industry. According to preliminary explorations, there was every indication of an unlimited supply of this fur bearing animal in what was soon to be called Nieuw Nederlant (New Netherlands).[20]

By the year 1624, the West India Trade Company had set up three trading posts in the interior of North America: High Island (in the Delaware River near Burlington,

New Jersey), Fort Orange (in Albany, New York), and Fort Hope (in Hartford, Connecticut, on the Connecticut River). In *The Iroquois*, Snow describes the vastness of the trade operation: "The Dutch had opened the equivalent of a modern megamall on the eastern edge of Iroquoia [the Iroquois land], and the Mohawks were closest to the new riches. . . . They anticipated the Dutch demand for beaver pelts."[21]

The relationship with the Dutch, however, got off to a bad start. The first director of the West India Trade Company, Daniel van Crieckenbeeck, was warned not to get involved in any Indian disputes, but he ignored advice and sided with a non-Iroquois tribe against the Mohawk.

The Mohawk, who outnumbered the Dutch, killed many settlers, along with their non-Iroquois allies, and the settlers moved out of the area, leaving only a handful of soldiers to maintain the post. A new Dutch negotiator, Pieter Barentsz, was able to assure the Mohawk that the battle did not signify the hostility of all Dutch people to the Mohawk. Gehring and Starna report, Barentsz was "not only able to pacify this Iroquois group, thus preventing retaliatory strikes against their vulnerable posts, but they also managed to establish a bond of mutual interest and friendship which was never broken."[22]

This same unwavering trust was not true of the Mohawk's relationships with

English explorer Henry Hudson offers a drink to a Mohawk leader. Hudson set up a fur-trading post in Mohawk territory near Albany, New York.

other Europeans, including the missionaries, who had only partial success in moving into Iroquois country, making friends with the native inhabitants, and converting them to Christianity.

Christian Missionaries

In the seventeenth century, French Jesuit priests were determined to bring the gospel to the New World. At first they avoided, as had many other missionaries, the land of the fierce Mohawk. But in 1642, Father Isaac Jogues and two other Jesuits went to the Mohawk village. Jogues's own notes provide a glimpse of missionary activity in the region: "There is no exercise of Religion except the Calvinist, and the orders declare that none but Calvinists be admitted; nevertheless, that point is not observed,—for besides the Calvinists, there are in this settlement Catholics, English Puritans, Lutherans, [and] Anabaptists."[23]

The Catholic missionaries represented mainly by Father Jogues and his Jesuit companions did not survive long in Mohawk territory. The two priests with Father Jogues were killed, and he was mutilated and enslaved. Father Jogues managed to escape with the help of the Dutch at Fort Orange, but he returned in 1646 when the authorities thought it was safe. On this trip, Father Jogues was successful as an ambassador to the Mohawk and left some of his belongings with them, planning to return to the Mohawk people as a full-time missionary after a trip to Canada. However, during Father Jogues's absence, a smallpox epidemic spread throughout the village. Superstitious and weakened by the illness, the Mohawk blamed the resulting deaths on the contents of a locked box Father Jogues had left behind. The Mohawk believed that the box contained evil spirits. When Jogues returned in September 1646, he was tortured and killed by the Mohawk. Nevertheless, Jesuits continued to return to the Mohawk region and preach.

In 1676, Kateri Tekakwitha, a young Mohawk woman influenced by the French Jesuit missionaries, was baptized as Roman Catholic. Harassed by the traditional Mohawk, she and other Christians moved to Caughnawaga on the St. Lawrence River in 1677. Kateri died three years later already legendary for her goodness.

Although the Mohawk treated the Jesuits very harshly by today's standards, in the context of seventeenth-century tribal culture, their actions were not extreme.

Types of Warfare

Historians specializing in the history of the Iroquois identify three different types of hostile encounters: feuding, raiding, and pitched battle. The Mohawk warriors engaged in all three. Feuding included violence between families, clans, and other groups linked politically to the village. Raiding was probably the most common form of conflict. It involved a group of between ten and one hundred men who might approach another settlement and attack or ambush people. Raiders often took scalps, captured women, and killed as many people as possible. Pitched battle was a disorganized clash between war parties of two hundred to two thousand men shooting arrows and engaging in one-on-one combat. Most of the time, there were few casualties.

During the sixteenth century, warfare with European settlers who invaded the Mohawk territory was common. Showing much more organization than was evident in tribal fighting, chiefs of warring tribes decided just what tactics would be used and when the war would begin. Keeping the enemy in suspense was part of the strategy. Many nights before the official start of war, the Mohawk sang angry war chants and danced around the fire. In *The Iroquois*, Snow gives a description of the scene:

> Setting the war kettle (or pot) of dog meat on the fire would at last initiate action. Speakers appealed to the sun for victory and captives, and asked for illumination of the path to and from the enemy. They promised to kill and eat their captives as sacrifices to the sun, or if nothing else to at least offer up a bear. Painted men sang furious songs, night after night until the time of departure. They left the village in their finest clothes, moving to the edge of the woods where they met the women carrying provisions and their travel clothes. After they left they would not be seen again until they returned and the leader made a thanksgiving feast.[24]

In his description of the New Netherlands, Adraien Van der Donck, a Dutch attorney in Albany in 1641, describes the weapons and preparation for warfare:

> Their weapons used to be, always and everywhere, bow and arrow, a war club on the arm and, hanging from the shoulder, a shield big enough to cover all of the body up to the shoulders. They paint and do up their faces in such a manner that they are barely recognizable even to those who know them well. Then they tie a strap of snakeskin around the head, fix a wolf's or fox tail upright on top and stride as imperiously as a peacock. Nowadays they make much use in their warfare of flintlock handguns, which they learn to handle very well, prize highly, and spare no money to buy in quantity at high prices from the Christians. With it they carry a light ax in place of the war club and so they march off.[25]

Since before the coming of the Europeans, it had been common practice among tribes to take prisoners during battle. Sometimes, the prisoners were treated cruelly or killed; other times, they were adopted into the clan to take the place of those lost in the conflict. Snow explains the usual procedure:

> Supposed wrongful deaths were avenged, and captives taken to replace lost loved ones. A raiding party could bring back both men and women, but men were more of-

A Jesuit missionary teaches Mohawk men about Christianity. Most of the Mohawk resisted the missionaries' attempts to convert them.

ten tortured and killed. Some, especially women, were adopted to take the places of recently lost relatives. This bestowal of citizenship entailed renaming the adoptee from a set of traditional names owned by the clan. The adoptee might even be given the name of the person(s) he was to replace, thus completing the change in identity.[26]

Members of other tribes could quickly turn hostile if it served their interests. The events surrounding a hunting expedition in which the Mohawk were successful and the Algonquian were not illustrate this situation.

Weapons of War

In *The League of the Iroquois*, Lewis Henry Morgan describes the Iroquois Nation's principal weapons of war.

Bow and Arrow

"Arrow heads made of chert, or flint, were so common that it is scarcely necessary to refer to them. Occasionally they are found with a twist to make the arrow revolve in flight. The Indian feathered his arrow for the same purpose."

The War Club

The Gajewa was "a heavy weapon, usually made of ironwood with a large ball of knot at the Head. It was usually two feet in length and the ball five or six inches in diameter. In close combat, it was a formidable weapon."

The Deerborn Warclub was "made of hard wood, carved and decorated with feathers. A sharp pointed deer's horn was inserted into the handle."

Tomahawk

"The tomahawk succeeded the war club as the rifle did the bow. They are made of steel, brass, or iron. The tomahawk is the emblem of war itself. To bury it, is peace; to raise it, is to declare the most deadly warfare."

Two widely used weapons of war: the Mohawk tomahawk (above, right), and the Mohawk war club (above, left.)

French explorer Samuel de Champlain and his Algonquan allies attack the Mohawk in 1609. The Mohawk's clubs and arrows were no match for European firearms.

Tribal Enemies

Pretending to be friendly to the Mohawk by day in order to learn hunting skills, jealous members of a neighboring Algonquan tribe, under cover of darkness, murdered six Mohawk hunters as they slept, stole venison that the Mohawk had killed and stored, and returned to their settlement. When the Mohawk woke the next day and discovered the killings and the theft, they realized that the Algonquian were to blame. After returning to their own village, the Mohawk told their tribesmen of the assassination. Angry outcries erupted. Trying to make peace with the angry Mohawk people, the Algonquan chiefs presented some small gifts to the families of the murdered persons. However, the Mohawk distrusted the Algonquian after that incident.

It was in this time of hostility that the French explorer Samuel de Champlain, who had settled in Quebec, explored south and west and became friendly with the Algonquan Indians. Without knowing the reason for the Mohawk tribe's anger against the Algonquian, Champlain sided with the Algonqiuan against the Mohawk. Setting up a post on the St. Lawrence River, he and the Algonquian encountered the Mohawk in July 1609. Up till this time, the Mohawk had used only war clubs and bows and arrows in pitched battle, but anticipating the action of Christian Dutch settlers, Champlain armed the Algonquian with firearms, which they did not hesitate to use against the Mohawk. Instantly, Mohawk chiefs died before the eyes of their tribesmen. This unequal battle was to have long-lasting effects on the relationship between the Mohawk and the French. The trouble between the two groups was far from over.

Sir William Johnson became a close friend and ally of the Mohawk.

Mohawk Loyalties

The New York Mohawk were close to Albany, the center of English power in America, and had been treated well by the British in repayment for aid against the French. Therefore, they were largely pro-British, and when England began to gain power over France in the struggle for colonial control, the Mohawk were in a strong position. After the surrender of the French to General Jeffrey Amherst in 1759, the British gained supremacy in Canada.

In 1763, the year French Canada was officially transferred into British hands by treaty, King George III of England signed a proclamation making the Apalachian Mountains the boundary of Indian Country. Now, the British had little need for the Mohawk alliance because they could travel freely, buy furs directly, and move about without threat of attack. As a result, the Mohawk bond with the British weakened. Moreover, dangers from the English-speaking American colonists were an ever-present threat.

The Mohawk and the American Revolution

With the onset of the American Revolution, the Mohawk found themselves divided. The division was among the Iroquois people themselves. The New York Mohawk still sided with the British, and the Onondaga, Cayuga, and Seneca were generally pro-English, but other Iroquois tribes, the Oneida and Tuscarora, were sympathetic to the American colonists. In *The Iroquois*, Snow explains how the split in loyalties shattered the invisible longhouse, the grouping of tribes from east to west forming the Iroquois League:

> The League Chiefs met in council, trying to find consensus, but the search was futile. An epidemic struck the assembly at Onondaga, killing three League Chiefs and many others. Finally, in 1777, as war raged between the English and the Americans, the League of the Iroquois covered the council fire at Onondaga. This action symbolically suspended the work of the league, with no promise that it would ever be resumed. No united Iroquois course of action was possible.[27]

Some of the chiefs who held to traditional beliefs that the league should be of one mind thought that the Iroquois should remain neutral during the war, but the actions of the colonists soon caused most Iroquois to join the British in the fight. Captain Dalton, the superintendent of Indian affairs for the United States, published an account on August 5, 1783, which stated the number of Indians from various tribes who fought for the British: "12,690 Indian Warriors were employed in the Revolutionary War; 300 were Mohawks."[28]

Few Mohawk supported the colonists. The number who did is unknown.

Joseph Brant and Sir William Johnson

Among the pro-British Mohawk warriors who fought during the Revolution was Joseph Brant. One of the most prominent men of the time, Joseph Brant was a Mohawk scholar, orator, translator, ambassador, and statesman, as well as a soldier. He emerged as a leader of his own people, acting as an arbitrator between the Mohawk and government authorities and commanding an Indian war party against the colonists. He became a close friend of Sir William Johnson, major general of the English forces.

Sir William Johnson came to the Mohawk valley from Ireland in 1737 as a young man of twenty-three to administer land for his uncle. Because of his honesty in dealing with the leading Indian chiefs and sachems, they adopted him as a full-fledged Mohawk chief, giving him the name Warraghiyagey, meaning "Chief Big Business." Johnson later became the royal commissioner for Indian affairs. He took the time to learn the Mohawk language and sat in on council meetings to find out about their decision-making process. Most important, Johnson stood up for the Indians to prevent them from being cheated in trade of furs and lands. He had a rare ability to persuade men to work together toward a common goal and was a good organizer.

After many years in America, Johnson's last act as royal commissioner was to call a meeting of six hundred Indians to his home to help plan a strategy to keep their territory. In failing health, Johnson spoke to the assembled group of tribesmen on the day of his death, July 11, 1774. After his speech, when he was being helped to his room, he told his good friend Joseph Brant, "Joseph, control your people. I am going away."[29] Johnson died two hours later.

Brant Alone

Since the American Revolution was being fought in what had been the Mohawk's territory, Johnson's concerns for the native people were well founded. Brant organized a special force of native and white Loyalist men called Brant's Volunteers. One of the most famous battles involving the Mohawk took place in Cherry Valley, New York, on November 11, 1778. Throughout the battle, Brant urged his men to be merciful, especially to women and children, and he saved the lives of many settlers. Campbell's account in the *Annals of Tryon County* records one such incident that illustrates Brant's concern for the colonists, whom the Mohawk people did not support.

As the story goes, Brant entered a house of one of the colonists and found a woman going about her everyday routine as though there was no war taking place just outside her door. Brant accused the woman of being involved.

"Are you thus engaged while all your neighbours are murdered around you?" . . . "We are King's people," she replied. "That plea will not avail you today." . . . "There is one Joseph Brant; if he is with the Indians he will save us." "I am Joseph Brant; but I have not the command, and I know not that I can save you; but I will do what is in my power." . . . Brant . . . gave a long shrill yell; soon after a small band of Mohawks were seen crossing the adjoining field with great speed. . . . He addressed them— "Where is your paint? here [sic], put my mark upon this woman and her children." . . . Each tribe had its mark, by which they and their prisoners were designated; most prisoners were thus marked. It was evidence that they were . . . claimed by some particular tribe, or individual—and wo [sic] to that person upon whom no captor had put his mark.[30]

In 1779 the Mohawk attack on Cherry Valley caused the American colonists to send out three expeditions under the leadership of Generals John Sullivan and James Clinton. When the colonists attacked the Mohawk, destroying their crops and villages, the outnumbered Native Americans had no choice but to flee. One group, the Upper Castle Mohawk, fled to Fort Niagara. Some of the tribe, mostly the Lower Castle Mohawk, went to Montreal. Others scattered into refugee villages

Joseph Brant

Joseph Brant, who took the name of Thayendanegea, was one of the most prominent Mohawk Indians in American and Canadian history, succeeding brilliantly in the world of the white man as well as in the world of the Mohawk. Brant was born on the banks of the Ohio River in 1742 while his parents were on a hunting expedition. However, he grew up in the Mohawk River Valley during a period of transition when Native Americans of the Northeast took on European cultural ways.

Sir William Johnson arranged for Brant and some other Mohawk youths to attend Moor's Indian Charity School in Connecticut, which was later moved to New Hampshire and became Dartmouth College. Brant's education prepared him to play a leading role in the frontier diplomacy of the 1790s.

At the age of twenty-six, Brant married the daughter of an Oneida chief and settled on a farm near Fort Canajoharie in Ontario, Canada. He became a devout Christian, and he and his wife had two children before her death in 1771.

Brant became chief of the confederacy of the six Iroquois nations in about 1776. Because of his leadership skills, he also received a captain's commission in the British army in charge of forces loyal to the Crown. Because of this position he traveled to England, where his education and cultured manners impressed many of the nobles.

Throughout his life, Brant encouraged moral improvement in the members of his tribe. On November 24, 1807, Brant died at his home on the Grand River reservation in Ontario and was buried beside the Episcopal church he had built near there.

Mohawk chief and British army captain Joseph Brant was at home in both the Indian and white cultures.

Kateri Tekakwitha

Among the Iroquois who converted to Christianity, the most famous was a Mohawk woman who may become the first North American Indian saint, Kateri Tekakwitha. The following excerpt from her biography can be found at Syracuse Online (www.syracuse.com):

"The daughter of a Christian Algonquin mother and a non-Christian Mohawk chief, Kateri was born on the south bank of the Mohawk River in a village known as Ossernenon. As a young woman, Kateri confided to a priest that she wanted to be baptized. She was so devoted to her faith she pledged a vow of perpetual virginity, alienating fellow Native Americans who hoped she'd marry. She spent what remained of her short life caring for the sick and teaching prayers to children until she died of illness at the age of 24.

Kateri has been declared blessed by the Vatican. This is the Roman Catholic Church's first step in declaring a holy person a "saint." But before Kateri can be called a saint, people must venerate her and miracles must be credibly attributed to her. A miracle is a happening that cannot be ex-plained by natural causes. Two miraculous happenings have already been credited to Kateri. In one case, prayers to Kateri were said to have made a deaf boy hear. In another, doctors wanted to remove a boy's eye because it was so badly injured, but after prayers to Kateri, the eye healed."

A shrine commemorates the life of Kateri Tekakwitha.

along the Pennsylvania line. Most of the tribe left their homes and fled to Canada.

Again, Joseph Brant looked for a way to help his people. This time the safest route seemed to be relocation. However, Brant also wanted his people to become more like the Europeans in their style of living and their way of thinking. Perhaps he saw this change as the only way to survive. In later years, he was criticized by some of his own people for selling off land and leasing sections to non-Indian tenants; they thought he betrayed his heritage.

Under the provisions of the 1783 Treaty of Paris that formally ended the Revolutionary War, the boundary of British territory in North America ran far north of the Mohawk River Valley along what is now the Canada–U.S. border in the Great Lakes region. Most of Brant's followers stayed along the shores of the Grand River. In 1785, the Crown granted land for six miles on either side of the Grand River to the Iroquois, which was the beginning of the Six Nations Reserve. Later, land disputes erupted, and the land that had been granted to the Iroquois was sold or leased to Britons.

Meanwhile, problems between the French and English continued, and the Mohawk again found themselves involved.

The French and English in Canada

By the provisions of the Canadian Articles of Capitulation and later the Quebec Act of 1763, the French who remained in Canada gained the right to retain their schools, practice the Catholic religion, and maintain the court system under French law. But by 1822, the British wanted to unite Canada under one rule. By this time, the Mohawk were not interested in the disagreements between the French and the British. They lived peacefully in small villages in homes hewn out of logs or built of stone. Trouble, however, came to them. French soldiers planned to hold a number of Mohawk men hostage; they wanted to raid a military supply house so that they could steal arms and attack the British. The quick thinking of one Mohawk woman managed to change the plans of the French and once again secure the peace and goodwill of the British toward the Mohawk people.

Throughout the seventeenth century, and into the eighteenth, the Mohawk people established new friendships, defended themselves against hostile tribes and European invaders, and survived the changing attitudes of people within their own tribe. They had to adopt new ways, but they sustained themselves as a people. Their bond with one another and the spiritual force of their beliefs in the Great Spirit continued.

Chapter 4

Ceremonies and Rituals

According to the Mohawk belief system, spiritual force came from the Great Spirit who created man and all useful elements on earth; he brought happiness and protection to the people. While the Great Spirit was responsible for all goodness, his twin brother, the Evil Spirit living in the land below, was responsible for all unhappiness. He created monsters and poisonous reptiles and plants. These twin spirits were destined to live an endless existence vying for power. Because the Mohawk were deeply spiritual people, they observed seasonal ceremonies, practiced shamanism in many forms, and were influenced by various religions.

Hertzberg in *The Great Tree and the Longhouse* explains the Iroquois's reverence for nature: "The physical environment of the Iroquois was infused with a religious and spiritual meaning. . . . In the Sky dwelt 'Our Grandmother the Moon' and 'Our Elder Brother, the Sun.' . . . The Corn Mother watched over the fields, and in the woods lived the Little People and the masked spirits."[31]

The Iroquois devoted many celebrations to honoring nature. Various parts of the rituals were standard from one celebration to the next. For example, the Mohawk always opened and closed each celebration with prayers of thanksgiving to the Great Spirit. During these prayers, objects near the earth such as rocks, trees, and flowers were mentioned, as were elements in the sky such as wind, thunder, the moon, stars, and the sun. The Mohawk burned tobacco leaves to symbolize that their message rose to the Great Spirit like the plumes of smoke given off by the burning plant. Wampum belts were brought out and used to record history or tell stories. During the day the mood was solemn, but at night the Mohawk enjoyed themselves. The changing of the seasons required special ceremonies of celebration for the Mohawk people.

Ceremonies of the Seasons

In the spring, soon after the first shoots of green appeared on the trees, the Mohawk gave thanks to the creator for the forest, par-

Iroquois Prayer of Thanksgiving

The following, from Joseph Bruchac's "A Mohawk Village in 1491," is a translation of an excerpt from the traditional Iroquois Prayer of Thanksgiving:

"We return thanks to our mother, the earth, which sustains us . . . to the wind, which, moving the air, has banished diseases . . . to our grandfather He-no, that he has protected his grandchildren . . . and has given to us his rain . . . to the sun, that he has looked upon the earth with a beneficent [kind] eye."

Today, the Iroquois Prayer of Thanksgiving is recited daily in the Mohawk language by students at the Freedom School in Akwesasne.

A drawing depicts Native Americans enacting a sacrificial ritual to the Great Spirit.

Medicine Bundle

Medicine men carried bundles with organic substances. Some common ingredients included animal hearts, dried snake blood, hair, powders, and grease. Dried animal parts were usually burned in ceremonial fires. There might also be fossils, crystals, or pebbles in the pouch. The medicine men used these items to ward off evil spirits. In *The Iroquois*, Dean Snow describes the method used by medicine men to arrive at a cure:

"The rite chosen to help a sick person is determined by what that person has dreamed. If he cannot remember a dream, then a shaman must be consulted to determine which rite to use. The dream, whether or not it is remembered, is thought to express subconscious desires. The Iroquois philosophy held that failure to act upon those desires is what has made the person sick to begin with."

Of all the objects used to bring about cures, human bones were thought to be the most powerful.

A typical shaman's medicine bundle. The contents of the bundle usually included animal parts, stones, and other objects considered to have spiritual power.

ticularly the maple. Because the tribe did not have refined sugar from cane, the syrup from the maple was their only sweetener.

The Green Corn Festival was usually held in August when the corn was ready to eat. It was a way for the Mohawk to honor the Corn Mother who had given them the crop. On the first day of the rituals, the clans named the children who had been born since the midwinter celebration. On the second day, the Mohawk people thanked the elements of nature close to them: berries on the bushes and crops in the fields. By the third day, they thanked each other for acts of kindness and celebrated by playing games. One of the most popular games was the bowl game, in which one moiety vied against another. After the fourth day of singing and playing games, the people of the Mohawk tribe turned to the harvest and the work of bringing in the food and storing it in the longhouses for the coming winter.

In the fall, when all the crops had been gathered, prepared, and stored for winter, the Mohawk celebrated the Harvest Festival to honor the "Three Sisters," corn, squash, and beans. The Mohawk placed these and many other crops under the watchful care of the protecting spirit. Like the Green Corn Festival, this celebration followed the pattern of beginning and ending with the thanksgiving speech and featured the burning of tobacco and the life supporter dances.

The Midwinter Festival was a time when the Mohawk people cleansed their spirits and their homes. In late January or early February, the Mohawk held a week-long ceremony. To start the festivities, the highest-ranking man in the household went from longhouse to longhouse stirring the ashes of the fires to announce the time of renewing by means of drums, dancing, and playing games. Because the Mohawk believed that dreams were important to physical health, they spent time during the midwinter festivities making up riddles and guessing each other's dreams. Then they offered suggestions to the dreamer about how these dreams might be fulfilled. As was common in all festivities, the Mohawk people offered thanksgiving to the Great Spirit during the celebration. One noteworthy practice of the midwinter ritual was to strangle two white dogs to honor the supernatural being. At the end of the festivities, one dog was burned to ask the great creator to protect the tribe during the new year. Part of the ceremony required each person to sing his or her personal song to renew the strength of the guardian spirit or protector.

All the babies who had been born since the Green Corn Festival in summer received names from their mother's clan during the Midwinter Festival. Others might also have a name change at this time. The concept of names held great significance for the Mohawk. In *The Great Tree and the Longhouse*, Hertzberg explains the importance and the custom of bestowing names:

> A name was thought to contain the thinking part of the soul. Around a

name would grow a kind of personality. . . . Moreover, an Iroquois had a number of names in the course of his life. He might be given one name when he was born, another when he reached adolescence, and another on some other occasion. When he got the new name he dropped the old one. . . . A number of Iroquois names were actually titles, and carried religious or political responsibilities.[32]

Closely related to ceremonies celebrating the seasons were the religious practices adopted from groups who influenced the Mohawk people. Although some Mohawk converted to Christianity as a result of the Jesuits' preaching, others wanted to retain their tribal customs. After a time, however, the people became lax in observing even these familiar practices. A fellow tribesman helped to renew their value system.

The Religion of Handsome Lake

At the turn of the nineteenth century, a Mohawk Indian named Handsome Lake (Skanyadariyoh) called his fellow tribesmen to reform. Handsome Lake, who was addicted to the use of alcohol, vowed to reform himself and renew tribal religious practices. Part of his desire to change came from Quaker influence; part was the result of a series of personal visions.

In 1799, Handsome Lake had the first of three visions. He collapsed and seemed to die, but when he awoke, he said he had a dream in which the spirit told him he must give up alcohol or die. In the second vision, he was given a tour of heaven and hell and received the "Good Message," which became the basis for a new moral code. In the final vision, he was told to reform the Midwinter Festival and add festivities. As a result, he put in place the Feather Dance, the Thanksgiving Dance, the Rite of Personal Chant, a game of chance called the bowl game, and lacrosse competitions, extending the ceremonies by four days.

After the encounters with the spirit in his visions, Handsome Lake was gradually cured of his desire for alcohol. He preached the message of reform to the Seneca and later to the other Iroquois tribes, who traveled many miles to hear him speak. His message stressed thanksgiving, appreciation for the goodwill of the supernatural, and attention to the meaning of dreams. Changes he brought about included encouraging men to take on farming duties, which had traditionally been women's work; replacing the longhouse community concept with the husband–wife bond; and preaching the concept of the nuclear family.

Handsome Lake's zeal for tribal revival prompted him to seek help from the U.S. government. Like Native Americans of other tribes, many Iroquois men had become alcoholics. In 1802, Handsome Lake wrote to the president, Thomas Jefferson, to beg for his aid in prohibiting the white man's sale of liquor to the Iroquois. In a lengthy address, Jefferson responded that he would cooperate with Handsome Lake's request by forbidding such sales. Handsome Lake's teaching of religious reform became known as the Code of Handsome Lake.

A combination of religious and ceremonial practices influenced the life of the Mohawk people and strengthened their ties to nature and one another. The shaman helped to fortify the traditional bonds of the people with the spirit world.

Shamanism

Shamanism is a religious belief in gods, ancestral spirits, and demons. In cultures that practice shamanism, the shaman is a member of the tribe who is believed to have special powers to communicate with the spirit world, to control events, and to interpret hidden meanings. Among the Mohawk, the shamans with the greatest powers were divine chanters. Each shaman had his or her own song. In the Iroquois language, the word for "song" and the word for "power" are the same. Sometimes a man inherited his song from his father or from someone in his mother's clan. Other songs belonged to the tribe as a whole.

Tribal instruments might be used to accompany the beat of the song. One of the instruments was the turtle rattle. It was considered sacred by some Mohawk because it was made from the head and tail of the snapping or box turtle. Wood splints reinforced the neck for a handle. Another instrument, the water drum, was used to keep the beat during tribal ceremonies and ritual curing.

Curing the Sick

In the Mohawk society, both men and women helped to cure disease. Different maladies demanded different approaches. Van der Donck, observing the Mohawk's method of treating illness, describes three different Mohawk cures:

The Sauna

Adriaen van der Donck, in Dean Snow's edited volume *In Mohawk Country*, describes the unusual "steamless" sauna used by the Mohawk people to care for their health.

"The sauna [used by the Iroquois] is made of clay, let into the ground, fully enclosed and fitted with a small door through which they can just pass. They heat a quantity of pebbles and shove them in, all around the sides. Then the patient sits down in the middle, quite naked, cheerful and singing, and endures the heat as long as he can. Emerging, he lies down in cold spring water. This method benefits them greatly, they declare, and is a sufficient remedy for various ailments."

A drawing depicts Iroquois shamans performing a healing ritual in a longhouse. Mohawk shamans relied on fasting, sweating, and herbal potions for their cures.

When something ails them, fasting is their cure and if that does not help they go into a sauna and sweat it all out. They do this mainly in the mild season of the year, and may drink some potion with it, though very little. . . . They have a cure for lingering sores and ulcers. . . . They do all of this with herbs, roots, and leaves from the land, having medicinal properties known to them, and not made into compounds.[33]

Because women worked with plants and herbs, they knew which plants helped certain complaints and prescribed them as medicine for healing. Several Europeans who observed the Mohawk's use of herbal remedies recorded accounts of successful treatments.

Cadwallader Colden, a physician, botanist, statesman, and friend of the Iroquois who studied Indian habits, mentions cures in his letters to other professionals:

The Mohawks told him [Colden] of a root which they chewed when they were 'quite faint with travel & fasting,' by which they found their spirits restored wonderfully. The Indian pokeroot according to reports . . . was a cure for 'cancer.' It could also 'banish corns in twenty-four hours.'[34]

Peter Kalm, a Swede who wrote of his travels in North America in the late sixteenth century, reported that an Indian woman on the Mohawk River told him about an Iroquois toothache remedy that used "ripe seed capsules of the Virginia anemone, which were rubbed in pieces so that they resembled cotton. They were then dipped in brandy and the bitterness of the seeds was responsible for the effects."[35]

French missionaries in the area also confirmed the therapeutic use of plants for cures and observed the medicinal effects of sassafras. The Indians pounded the leaves of this tree and used the mixture to heal wounds of all kinds in a short time. Another Frenchman, Joseph-Francois Lafitau, mentions a Mohawk woman's use of the ginseng root. She "cured herself next day of an intermittent fever which had been plaguing her for several months."[36]

Medicine Men

When herbal remedies did not produce the desired cure, specialists known as medicine men were called in to minister to the sick. This practice reached its height during the seventeenth century (1634–1635) when the smallpox epidemic invaded longhouse communities. In his book *The Iroquois*, Snow describes how a person became a member of this special healing group:

Members of a medicine society are recruited by being cured by the society or by dreaming that they should join. One might also in some sense inherit membership or be recommended by a clairvoyant. Thus each society probably began as a single shaman who recruited apprentices by curing them or by being charismatic enough to appear in their dreams. . . . Members of the society meet at midwinter, and once

or twice a year to go through houses to cure illnesses.[37]

In exchange for tobacco or food, healers would try to take away illness from a suffering clan member. The Iroquois myth of a village headman who challenged the creator and later became known as "Old Broken Nose" or "Our Defender, the Doctor," gives insight about how the concept of the medicine man began. Hazel Hertzberg writes:

One day, when the earth was new, he [the headman] and the Creator had met and argued as to who controlled the earth. They agreed to settle the matter by having a contest to see who could move a distant western mountain. They sat down with their backs to the west, facing the east, holding their breaths. First the . . . [headman] called the mountain, which moved only a short way. Then the Creator summoned the mountain, which came directly to them. Meanwhile the headman smashed his nose against the mountain. That is why [he is depicted with] his nose broken and his mouth distorted with pain. The Creator, realizing that the challenger had great power, assigned him the task of driving disease from the earth and of helping the hunters. And the loser agreed to lend his power to humans if they would call him "grandfather," make offerings of tobacco, set down kettles of mush, and make masks which were his portrait.[38]

This legend apparently is the origin of the tradition of medicine men wearing face masks. The use of the face masks was widespread by the early eighteenth century. In 1724, the French missionary Lafitau witnessed the Midwinter Festival and mentioned that the Mohawk were wearing masks "made of true bark, or from a sack pierced for the eyes and mouth. . . . In this costume they [the Mohawk] run like madmen from house to house, breaking, destroying, and overthrowing everything, without anyone's finding this a procedure to be criticized."[39]

In his journal, Harmen van den Bogaert, who visited the Mohawk River Valley, gives an eyewitness account of medicine men at work:

> As soon as they arrived, they began to sing, and kindled a large fire, sealing the house all around so that no draft could enter. Then both of them put a snakeskin around their heads and washed their hands and faces. They then took the sick person and laid him before the large fire. Taking a bucket of water in which they had put some medicine, they washed a stick in it ½ ell long [about 13 inches]. They stuck it down their throats so that the end could not be seen, and vomited on the patient's head and all over his body. Then they performed many farces with shouting and rapid clapping of hands, as is their custom, with much display, first on one thing and then on the other, so that sweat rolled off them everywhere.[40]

Although the patients sometimes recovered after these attempts to drive away evil spells or sickness, the cures were not always successful. Death was a frequent visitor to the Mohawk villages. The average life span of the Mohawk was thirty-one years.

Ceremonies for the Dead

Just as there were rituals surrounding cures, there were also prescribed ceremonies for burial. Historian Gilbert Hagerty describes the scene archaeologists found in the seventeenth-century portion of a burial site at the Mohawk and Oneida excavation at Sand Hill:

> The youth of this village went down early with the contagion of the time [1634–1635] to be flexed [knees bent] and frozen in the sand. Mere infants comprising over one third of the entire number had not come far from their days of swaddling in cattail down, and over another third were young teen-age lads who could no longer carry out their chores of gathering fresh water clams and setting their nets for fish below the river rifts. Their sisters hardly had time to stain their fingers with picking the favorite blackberries of the yellow mandrake that abound in the nearby woods.[41]

While the death of the young was especially sad, the mourning of all who died was the responsibility of the surviving clan members. The opposite moiety respected the grief of the mourners and took charge of the preparation and burial of the body, which usually followed a prescribed order. For example, a deceased man was dressed in his best clothes, and his face painted. His bow and arrows, tobacco, and pipe, all of which were necessary for the journey to the afterlife, were placed beside him in the grave. The journey from earth to heaven took many days. Some believed maybe a year. On the one-year anniversary of the death of a clan member, a special feast was held.

The specifics of burial, however, could vary from one village to the next. In *The League of the Iroquois*, Morgan gives his observations of burial procedures:

One possible posture for burial was [placing the corpse] sitting upright in the grave facing east with a gun barrel resting on the shoulder. Another procedure was to expose the body on a scaffolding until it wasted away on the skeleton. The bones were then removed to the house of the deceased or a small bark house nearby. In that way, the bones of families were kept together. If the family moved, the bones were collected and buried in a common site arranged in horizontal layers forming a conical pyramid.[42]

But there are also accounts that suggest that burial rituals may have been eliminated

A modern Mohawk medicine man wears a traditional "Old Broken Nose" mask while performing a ritual in the snow.

A nineteenth-century drawing depicts a Mohawk burial ritual. Some Mohawks buried their dead in a sitting posture.

altogether when large numbers of bodies were to be buried at the same time.

In his journal, van den Bogaert describes the external appearance of graves:

Just before reaching the castle [longhouse], we saw three graves in the manner of our graves: long and high. Otherwise their graves are round. These graves were surrounded with palisades that they had split from trees, and were so neatly made that it was a wonder. They were painted red, white, and black. Only the chief's grave had an entrance, above which stood a large wooden bird surrounded by paintings of dogs, deer, snakes, and other animals.[43]

Although the methods the clan used to honor and bury the dead may have varied from one longhouse community to another, great attention was given to the remains of all tribal members. In keeping with religious and ceremonial practices, the spirit world influenced the life—and death—of the Mohawk people, kept them well, and strengthened their ties to nature and one another. Pride in their culture and a love for the land were rooted deeply in the Mohawk way of life. This way of life would soon face a number of challenges.

Chapter 5

Lost Lands and New Lifestyles

Just as the American colonists were gaining their independence, it became very clear that Native Americans were losing their freedom. As a result of warfare in the late eighteenth and nineteenth centuries, segments of the Mohawk community were forced by the governments of the United States and Canada to relocate and adopt new ways of living.

The Mohawk in the United States

Mohawk people living in the United States encountered problems with the federal government and the governing body of New York. Most of the problems were about landownership. On the part of the Native Americans, the difficulty came from the fact that the whole concept of landownership was foreign to them. Believing that land belonged to everyone, the Native Americans had trouble understanding a legal system in which parts of the earth could be bought and sold.

In addition to the different ways of thinking about landownership, entering into legal agreements about property had many problems. There were constant arguments and misunderstandings about the sale of land. Sometimes the Mohawk land was sold without a contract, a practice allowing dishonest realtors to sell the same tract of land more than once. At other times, the person authorizing the sale had no authority to do so.

Problems with the Government of New York

Moreover, in 1783, lawmakers in the state of New York declared that the legislators themselves had the right to decide the fate of the Indians living there. With their British friends no longer able to offer protection, the Mohawk feared reprisals from the Americans. Armed attack was not the Mohawk's main problem, however. Government dealings were generally unfavorable and hard to understand. For example, Governor James Clinton seemed to be protecting Iroquois land rights at a meeting in Fort Stanwix, New York, in 1784. However, he was really denying the sale of Mohawk land to individuals, therefore setting the stage for the state of New York to later profit from the sale of the same land.

Problems with the Federal Government

Not only were representatives from the state of New York eager to claim Iroquois land, the federal government was also organizing to take over Native American interests. After the Revolutionary War, the new government of America was deciding what powers should belong to the states and what powers should be held by the federal government. Part of the federal government's job of uniting the colonies meant finding a solution to the "Indian problem."

To manage Indian affairs, the new Constitution, which began functioning in 1789, forbid states from entering into treaties, alliances, or confederations with Indian tribes. In 1789, the U.S. War Department was created, and one of the tasks assigned to this new group was Indian affairs. Anthropologist Peter Nabokov explains the significance of this action: "For the next quarter century, until the Bureau of Indian Affairs was transferred to the Department of the Interior, the Indian 'problem' was considered a military matter."[44] Leaders of the new nation knew all too well the cost of war.

The Treaty of Big Tree

The Revolutionary War had been expensive for the government of the new country. The federal government of the young American nation believed that the sale of land would be a convenient way to pay for the war. Robert Morris, one of the colonists who had helped finance the war, was in desperate need of money. He owned land in New York State, which he had bought from the Commonwealth of Massachusetts. In order to pay his bills, he decided to sell the land to a group of wealthy merchants in Amsterdam who had friends in America willing to act on their behalf. One large problem with completing the sale was the fact that the Indians still held ownership of the land. Morris had to secure rights to the land in order to sell it to the Holland Land Company. After many unsuccessful tries with the Seneca, he contacted President Washington and asked for a commissioner of the federal government to preside at a treaty with the Seneca Nation. In this way, Morris could formally transfer control of the land to the Holland Company without the problem of settlers squatting on the land and claiming rights to it later.

President Washington sent Colonel Jeremiah Wadsworth to act as a commissioner at the formal meeting with the Seneca people at Big Tree on September 15, 1797. Fifty-two Seneca, including chiefs and sachems, signed the treaty. The terms of the Treaty of Big Tree gave the Seneca money and the right to keep some land. It stated that the Seneca would receive payment of $100,000 for a portion of their landholdings "to be vested in the stock of the bank of the United States, and held in the name of the President of the United States for the use . . . of the said nation of Indians."[45] In addition, certain tracts of land would be "laid off" near the existing villages to be held in "reserve" for the use of the tribe. In *The Iroquois*, Snow summarizes the land agreement that resulted from the treaty and its impact on the Iroquois: "They [the government with the

approval of the chief or sachem near the area] reserved 310 square miles in eleven tracts, seven of them very small areas scattered mostly along the Genesee River. . . . It was the beginning of the reservation system."[46]

The Holland Land Company hired Joseph Ellicott to survey the land tracts and lay out the boundaries for Seneca reservations. His

In 1797, Robert Morris initiated a land treaty with the Seneca. The treaty established the first Indian reservation.

Lewis H. Morgan

As an adopted member of the Iroquois Confederacy, Lewis Henry Morgan spent much of his adult life learning the habits and customs of these Native Americans, which he then passed on to scholars through his writings.

Lewis H. Morgan was born in 1818 in Aurora, New York. From his youth, Morgan was known as an organizer. At a young age he started a boys' club to read the classics. Later he went on to Union College in Schenectady and became a lawyer in upstate New York. He spent a great deal of time learning the customs of the Iroquois people and meeting with their chiefs. In 1847, Governor John Young asked Morgan to gather artifacts for the Cabinet of Natural History in Albany. Although some scholars have questioned the accuracy of his early written work, Morgan later wrote the first authentic account of the Iroquois tribes, "League of the Ho-de-no-sau-nee," in 1851. When Morgan died in 1881, the fame he had earned for his studies and his writings led other scholars to call him the Father of Anthropology.

Lewis H. Morgan wrote extensively on Iroquois life and customs.

work was completed in October 1800. Some of the Seneca moved to the tracts of lands allotted to them or joined remnants of dislocated tribes; others decided to move west. For those who chose to stay on the reservations, their living spaces were cramped, and sickness and disease were a constant problem as they battled smallpox and yellow fever. For the Seneca and other Iroquois nations, their tribes were further split by the encroachment of settlers in nearby areas.

Other land companies followed the Holland Company, buying up territory once belonging to the Iroquois, and fraudulent contracts robbed the tribes of more and more land. By the late nineteenth century, there was no more Indian territory to dispute. Land that once belonged to the

Iroquois had been lost through government force, bribery, or sale, legally or illegally. In addition to the loss of their land, the Iroquois people were presented with another threat: the loss of their culture.

Stamping Out the Culture

In 1887, the American government passed the Dawes General Allotment Act. This legislation, which defined the direction of the federal Indian policy for generations, was to have disastrous effects on Native Americans everywhere. Snow outlines the provisions of the act:

Indians were to be integrated into Euro-American society. Policy makers thought that the way to achieve this was to encourage the speaking of English, conversion to Christianity, and the pursuit of Euro-American livelihoods wherever possible. Allotment of reservation lands to individuals was designed to break up traditional political institutions and to encourage the growth of family farms in the Euro-American tradition.[47]

Thus, the Dawes Act facilitated the government policy of stamping out Native American culture. There were other unfavorable developments, as well: The U.S. government was not helpful in maintaining the security of the Iroquois Nation, and the Canadian government presented problems of its own.

The Iroquois and the Canadian Government

By 1700, two-thirds of all Mohawks were living in Canada. The Canadian government, backed by powerful interest groups, had its own ideas about how to deal with the new residents.

By the mid–eighteenth century, the French, who still maintained a great deal of influence in Canada, persuaded the Indians from the various missionary settlements to unite. So the Mohawk who had sided with the French, together with the Algonquian, Nipissing, Caughnawaga, Onondaga, and Cayuga, formed a confederation. The Catholic religion was their common bond.

The Canadian government posed problems for the Mohawk way of life. In 1842, the Bagot Commission decided that the best way to address the difficulties with the Native Americans was to turn them into Canadian citizens. So in keeping with the commission's recommendations, the Canadian Parliament developed a series of laws. Between 1850 and 1867, it passed several laws that gave Canadian citizenship to native people who wanted it; however, by becoming a Canadian citizen, a Native American ceased to belong to a tribe. In addition to the legislation recommended by the Bagot Commission, other legislation followed, which spelled out the intentions of the government.

According to Mohawk historian David Blanchard in *Seven Generations*, the Indian Act of 1876 had several goals: "to weaken the power and prestige of traditional native government, to remove women of the nation from positions of power, to give native people Canadian citizenship, and to gradually terminate all claims of native people to land in Canada."[48] The Act of 1876 was amended in 1879 and again in 1884 in attempts to encourage the Mohawk people to reject their tribal affiliation. As a reward for assuming Canadian citizenship, the government promised to train the Native Americans for government positions. The Mohawk, however, suspected that the government would ensure that any Indians who obtained a government job would never rise to power. The Mohawk's suspicions about the Canadian government proved true. The legislature soon took steps to replace the twelve hereditary chiefs with an equal number of elected officials. According to Snow, "This newly appointed council was called the 'band council.' It meant that the hereditary chiefs were ignored by the government."[49]

The Mohawk Nation Responds

The Mohawk people were not happy with the actions and policies of the Canadian government, which was not only taking away their land but also trying to take away the ability of the people to govern themselves. Their response to government interference, according to Blanchard, was a reminder of previous agreements that had been broken: "It recalled promises the British made to 'remain in its own vessel and the native in his birch bark canoe,' and that the British will never make any compulsory laws for the Six Nations and the treaties between them shall remain unmolested forever."[50]

The Indians petitioned the government to be consulted about decisions that affected them as a people, but to no avail. The Canadian government decided to carry out its original plan of making the Indians citizens. The Indians decided to protest. In 1890, the Canadian Mohawk signed their names to a petition and sent it to the governor general of Indian affairs. T.M. Daly, who was the superintendent of Indian affairs, went with his deputy to try to persuade the Kahnawake people at a general meeting to accept the thinking of the Canadian government. When this meeting did not end with the results Daly wanted, the people of the Kahnawake reserve waited one more year before petitioning the new minister of Indian affairs, Clifford Sifton, with the same plea.

This time, Mohawk women appealed. Blanchard shares their written message:

> We are simply women, but it is our confidence of our noble and gracious mother, the Queen [Victoria] of England, who, being a woman, and recalling to mind that your mother was also a woman . . . kindly hear our words of petition, and do not despise the words and voice of a woman. . . . Since the change of our chiefs, into councilors, our sorrows manifolded, we have lost many advantages, it has caused many family disputes, brother against brother. It has separated them and it has caused an ill feeling which is yet burning.[51]

The women's words were ignored. In 1898 the Mohawk women again wrote to the governor general. They received a short message that said they were "in defiance"

Eli Parker

Eli Parker's name is often remembered in connection with Lewis Henry Morgan, Handsome Lake, and General Ulysses Grant, but he was important in his own right, too.

A Seneca born on a Tonawanda reservation in 1825, Parker was educated at a Baptist mission school with white children. Because he learned English very well, he later became a translator and scribe of legal documents for his tribe. In 1845, Parker became the first person to make a written record of the teachings of Handsome Lake.

After traveling to Albany, New York, Parker met Lewis Morgan. The two became friends because each shared knowledge the other valued. Parker wanted to know U.S. law, and Morgan was a lawyer; Morgan was fascinated with the study of people and their customs, especially the Iroquois, and Parker was a Seneca.

As a friend of General Ulysses Grant, Parker was given the honorary title of brevet brigadier general and became his aide. Parker was present at the surrender at Appomattox and later appointed commissioner of Indian affairs.

Seneca Indian Eli Parker became a general in the Union army and an aide to Ulysses Grant.

A steamship sails the Lachine Rapids of Canada's St. Lawrence River. Many Mohawk men deftly piloted such ships through the treacherous rapids.

as gradual as the loss of land itself. The removal of the Mohawk and other native tribes in small isolated areas forced the people to act independently of each other. No longer did they have the sense of oneness of the tribe and the unity of the longhouse community. As scholar William Fenton observes, "When a pattern of culture is shattered, the people lose their vital spark. The Iroquois had long done things in common and with unanimity, and it was the abandoning of this principle . . . that led directly to the loss of their land."[52]

With the loss of land and the sense of oneness, the traditional concept of the male as hunter and warrior was gone. Restricted from moving about freely to hunt, fish, trap, and defend the longhouse, the men now had to survive by earning a living in the white man's world. Fenton explains what the loss of identity did to the Mohawk's morale:

> Unemployed warriors frequented the taverns that sprang up at Buffalo [a city in central New York near the Canadian border], nearly everyone drank to excess when he could obtain spirits, and the disorganization of the

of the government of Canada. Although the Indians were technically in a state of revolt, there was little they could do to defend their cause against a government power.

A Pattern Is Shattered

The effects of the government takeover of Native American landholdings in the United States, as well as in Canada, were culture was apparent to Indians and white observers alike.[53]

Change of Occupation

Bound to the Euro-American ideas of culture, some of the Mohawk men became depressed. Others looked for jobs away from their villages. In Canada, a number of men relocated to other provinces to find employment as trappers and traders with local companies. Others worked as voyagers (river pilots), steering steamers, rafts, and boats filled with cargo or passengers over the treacherous Long Sault Rapids near Cornwall and the Lachine Rapids near Lachine, both in Canada.

The most treacherous rapids were the Lachine. Few river pilots had the courage to take large ships through the swirling waters. But Blanchard mentions that Mohawk men seemed particularly skilled at the job:

Many Kahnawake men became famous as river pilots on the Lachine Rapids. Two that are remembered are Kahonwasene (Big John Canadian) and Kanatsiohare (John Patton). Some of these men worked the lower St. Lawrence, carrying mostly passengers over the Lachine Rapids. Others worked the upper St. Lawrence and Ottawa Rivers carrying freight, logging barges and other raw materials into the port of Montreal to be shipped overseas on large vessels.[54]

But river boating and fur trading were

not for everyone. Some men chose to work in the logging camps near Elk Lake, Ontario.

New Opportunities

By 1862, another opportunity for Mohawk men in search of work presented itself. The Civil War raging in America needed soldiers. Although Indians were not considered citizens and could not apply for citizenship, they could fight in wars and receive the same pay as Europeans and Americans.

In *The Iroquois*, Snow explains the Mohawk's desire to serve in the army:

Army service provided the outlet that combat had always given the Iroquois. It was time away from . . . reservation life and the tensions of ever-present factional disputes. It was also a source of cash for young men having little other access to it.[55]

The growth of railroads also presented job opportunities during the nineteenth century. The need for bridges to span the St. Lawrence River was another source of work. In 1850, the Grand Trunk Railway hired a British engineer to supervise the bridge-building project. In *Seven Generations*, Blanchard explains how the Kahnawake men became involved: "One of [British engineer James] Hodges' assistants suggested to him that Kahnawake was a good source for stone. There was a small quarry in the village at the time. Hodges decided to visit Kahnawake and talk to the chiefs."[56]

As a result of Hodges's visit, not only was the quarry chosen as a site to obtain stone, but the Kahnawake men were soon hired to transport stone from the Kahnawake quarry to the work location. Eventually, many of them were employed as construction workers to build the bridge. During the construction of the Victoria Bridge, the Mohawk men gained a reputation across Canada as high-construction workers (those who are skilled at doing ironwork in high places). New building jobs were soon open to the Mohawk men, and they were hired across Canada to build railway bridges.

In August 1860, when the Victoria Bridge was nearing completion, the Prince of Wales, Queen Victoria's husband, Albert, was invited from Great Britain to be present at the celebration opening the bridge for commercial use. Blanchard describes how the Mohawk men entered into the festivities at the home of Sir George Simpson, governor of the Hudson Bay Company: "Seventy-six men from Kahnawake crossed the lake dressed in feathers and war paint. Paddling ten huge birch bark canoes, they performed maneuvers of water skills that dazzled the audience."[57] At the time, the Mohawk men did not

Construction workers pose at the site of the Victoria Railway Bridge in Montreal, Canada. Mohawk men helped build this bridge and gained a reputation for their ability to work at great heights.

Benjamin Franklin

As a scientist, statesman, Indian commissioner, and public servant, Pennsylvanian Benjamin Franklin helped to mold the political culture of the young United States. In the pre-Revolutionary period, when he and his friends were advocating a federal union of the colonies, no European model was found suitable. Some historians think that Franklin's connections with the Iroquois Confederacy may have given him valuable insights.

In 1744, the Iroquois leader Canassatego addressed colonial legislators in Philadelphia. Canassatego suggested that each colony have its own government, but together the thirteen speak with one voice to other nations. Few colonists were willing to listen to what the Indians had to say. But Franklin had studied the Indians and respected their ideas. As early as 1754, Franklin wanted to try Canassatego's idea and suggested uniting the colonies as one.

know it, but another opportunity for work was to result from their audience appeal. They would soon become international celebrities.

European Connections

Because an account of the events that took place in Canada was published in the London papers, stories of the Native Americans spread across the Atlantic Ocean. Europeans wanted to see demonstrations of the native tribes for themselves. The popularity of the Kahnawake's performances led to their visiting Europe to demonstrate their skills as entertainers. The Universal Exposition in Paris in 1867 gave the Mohawk entertainers the opportunity to attend the World's Fair. As it turned out, this was the first of several trips the Mohawk made to cities in Europe to exhibit their talents to world audiences.

In 1876, Queen Victoria invited some of the Mohawk people for a demonstration of lacrosse and dancing at Windsor Castle.

With celebrities as their audience, it did not take long for the Mohawk people to become active in the entertainment business. Among the most famous performers from Akwesasne were Jim "Running Deer" and his two brothers. As trick horse riders, they staged stunts to delight the audiences. Neither Jim's title, "the last hereditary chief of the Iroquois," nor the stagecoach robberies the group pretended to act out were actually part of the Mohawk life experience. Jim gave the people in the audience what they came to see. The men dressed in clothing and performed acts that were not really part of their tradition in order to earn money.

The transatlantic entertainers were contributors to early vaudeville in England

and on the Continent. Mohawk women and children were sometimes part of the performances too. In addition, they also made costumes and souvenirs to sell to the spectators after the shows. Blanchard gives insight into the result of this new occupation:

> One of the negative effects of the entertainment business was that the Mohawk people started to believe that the show songs, dances, and costumes were part of traditional Mohawk culture. Soon, people began to forget songs, dances and clothing of the Kanien'kehake [People of the Flint].[58] Others questioned the value of the money they earned compared to the harm of acting out stories that were the heritage of another tribe.

As the twentieth century approached, the Iroquois tribes were a people in transition. They had lost most of their land. It seemed that some had also lost a belief in traditions. That idea filled some of the Mohawk with a great deal of pain; others saw the loss as a necessary change in a modern world.

Chapter 6

The Mohawk in the Twenty-First Century

Many years have passed since the Mohawk were a dominant force in the area that is now New York State. Nevertheless, today the Mohawk tradition lives on in their territories in the United States and Canada. Concerns about education, occupations, and government relations remain uppermost in their daily life. According to the Mohawk Nation Council of Chiefs, the most populous Mohawk reservation sites are Akwesasne, Kahnawake, Kanesatake, Tyendinaga, and Wahta. A closer look at the separate areas reveals their histories as well as their similarities and differences.

Kanesatake

Kanesatake is a Mohawk reserve in Quebec that dates as far back as 1714, and archaeologists say maybe much longer. Its name means "Place of the Crusty Sand." The Mohawk people occupied this territory ever since King Louis XIV of France gave the tract of land to a religious order, the Sulpicians. Many Mohawk, Algonquian, and Nipissing all lived there at one time. According to current information from the Kanesatake Cultural Centre, "Kanesatake was an ideal location for a trade center, the Hudson's Bay Company even set up a trading post here,"[59] which is still standing.

Today, approximately seventeen hundred Mohawk live in Kanesatake. In April 1990, the people's struggle to retain the territory made news again. The residents of the town of Oka, Quebec, which is next to the Mohawk reservation, decided to expand their golf course. The Mohawk people objected, knowing the expansion would extend on to the reservation. The argument between the townspeople and the Indians led to an armed standoff. On July 11, one police officer was killed. Mohawk from other reservations came to help their fellow tribesmen set up a barricade. After much negotiation, the federal government purchased the disputed land, and the barricades were removed. In December 2000, the Canadian minister of Indian affairs, Robert Nault, and the chief of the

Mohawk dressed for battle blocked plans for building a golf course at Kanesatake in 1990.

Mohawk at Kanesatake James Gabriel, signed a historic agreement on land governance. It recognized the Kanesatake people's right to control their own territory. Kanesatake's revolt against the people of Oka was a modern-day chapter in the Mohawk's fight for justice.

Wahta Reserve

Located in central Ontario, the Wahta Reserve is a small community of Mohawk founded in 1881. The original members, who left because of civil and economic differences, were from Oka, Quebec.

According to the Bureau of Indian Affairs, today there are about 550 Mohawk at the Wahta Reserve. Programs for the Mohawk there include education, economic development, children's services, and a library. There is also a health and wellness program that operates from the Family Resource Center. The Wahta Mohawk participate in a traditional farming occupation. They own and operate Ontario's largest cranberry farm. On marshy, nutrient-rich land called a bog, they grow acres of cranberries. Nearby plant facilities turn out cranberry products such as juice and sauces. The bog is open to visitors.

Tyendinaga

The Mohawk at Tyendinaga, which means "Placing the Wood," live on the north shore of the Bay of Quinte on Lake Ontario. This land came to the Mohawk people from the British Crown as compensation for the tribe's losses after the American Revolution. Captain John Deserontyon, a Mohawk serving in the British army, selected the area. As early as 1784, about twenty Mohawk families claimed this territory. Originally, the tract of land was approximately 92,700 acres. Gradually, the Mohawk had to surrender some of the land, so today the reserve is only about 18,000 acres. One special landmark located there is Christ Church, which was built in 1843 to replace the original log church. It stands as a symbol of the tribe's relationship with the Church of England, the Anglican Church.

New construction on the reservation includes the Quinte Mohawk School (from kindergarten to eighth grade), which educates children who live on the land. Teachers designed special programs for the school, including Mohawk language classes at all grade levels, help for special needs students, arts and crafts programs, and Mohawk dancing. A new day-care facility is also part of the school. Ka:nhiote, meaning "rainbow" in English, is the name of Tyendinaga's library. Besides books, newspapers, and magazines, there is also a special collection of materials pertaining to Native American themes and authors. A health center and elders' lodge on the reservation serves the needs of some residents. The people of Tyendinaga also enjoy parks with baseball diamonds and a lacrosse box so that children can learn the traditional game.

The Mohawk Pledge

The Mohawk Nation of Akwesasne has a website (www.peacetree.com) for the *Six Nation Museum of Onchioto* that displays its sacred pledge in English.

"I pledge allegiance to true Indianhood and will never allow the Good Name of our ancient forefathers to be trampled into the dust. We turn back five centuries for our examples and act accordingly to the uprightness displayed by our ancestors at that time, let us honor and revere the memory of them by setting a good example."

Each year, dressed in native costume and enjoying a feast of traditional food, the Mohawk commemorate the founding of the Tyendinaga settlement with a reenactment of the canoes landing on the shore. Today, about eight thousand Mohawk reside in the territory.

A Mohawk father and son in traditional dress attend an outdoor Christian Eucharist in Canada. The Mohawk and the Anglican Church have learned to live in peace and cooperation.

Kahnawake

Just south of Montreal, Quebec, is the village of Kahnawake. After a massacre in 1690 at Lachine, the Mohawk people moved farther upstream. In 1716, they relocated in the Kahnawake reserve. The St. Lawrence Seaway Project sponsored by the Canadian government caused problems for the Mohawk between 1955 and 1959. The provincial authorities seized 1,260 acres of the Kahnawake reserve in order to construct a canal bypass around the Lachine Rapids. As a result, a section of the village that had been Mohawk land for more than two hundred years was destroyed. Angered by the loss, the Mohawk, represented by Chief Matthew Lazare, complained to the United Nations Human Rights Commission that the only compensation the Mohawk were being offered was monetary and that the suggested dollar amount was less than the compensation received by nearby non-Indian landowners.

Unfair treatment on many other issues prompted

Mohawk Ironworkers See Terrorist Plane Pass By

On September 12, 2001, Jim Adams, a writer for *Indian Country*, a leading Native American news source, wrote:

"Hogansburg, N.Y. Mohawk ironworkers were working 50 floors up . . . when an airliner passed within what seemed like 50 feet of their crane on the way to the World Trade Center about ten blocks away. Richard Otto immediately got on his cell phone with . . . Ironworkers Local at the St. Regis Mohawk Reservation. . . . As they were talking the second plane came by headed for the World Trade Tower. In addition to the immediate impact . . . the community had a sentimental attachment to the Twin Towers. Quite a few Mohawk men from Akwesasne actually helped to build the World Trade Center.

In a follow-up article, the same news source reported that the Mohawk of Akwesasne drove a vanload of supplies and a donation of $11,000 to New York in support of the rescue efforts at the World Trade Center."

The last cranes are lowered from the nearly finished south tower of New York's World Trade Center in 1971. Mohawk ironworkers were among those atop the towering structure.

the Mohawk of Kahnawake to create their own police force. For a time, the separate Mohawk law enforcement agency seemed to work. However, during the 1990s, many confrontations occurred between the Canadian police and the Mohawk law enforcement group. The Mohawk people felt they had a right to have their own officers empowered to settle reservation problems.

Today's Mohawk police force is known as the Peacemakers.

For the most part, though, the people of Kahnawake live in peace. They have created a cultural center and tourist attractions such as a bed and breakfast, gift shops, a bingo hall, restaurants, and batting cages. The Kateri Tekakwitha School in Kahnawake honors the virtuous, young

Mohawk maiden who died at an early age. Kateri is now venerated as "blessed," and she is being considered by the Vatican as a candidate for sainthood.

Akwesasne or Saint Regis

Akwesasne means "Land Where the Partridge Drums Its Wings." This territory has belonged to the Mohawk people since May 31, 1796, when the U.S. government established the reservation. The Saint Regis Mohawk Reservation covers an area of six square miles at the corner of Franklin County in the state of New York. The region is located along the St. Lawrence River where upstate New York intersects with Ontario and Quebec, Canada. Today, buildings on the reservation include tribal administrative offices, a health clinic, a senior citizens' community center, and a Head Start education building. About two

hundred new housing units have been added with funds from the government. Privately owned companies provide electric and telephone services to the residents. The tribe has its own waterline and sewer system. As far as communication within the reservation, two newspapers are published weekly and a radio station operates seven days a week. Public transportation is available to the Mohawk community. The health service has a station wagon to shuttle patients to the clinic, and a van transports seniors to the nutrition center and to shopping areas.

Akwesasne has a population of approximately seven thousand Mohawk people; the U.S. Census Bureau report for the year 2000 states that there are about 2,690 people on the American side of the reservation. In 1960, there were about the same number of people under the age of eighteen as over.

Greenpeace and Akwesasne

Greenpeace is an independent agency that is dedicated to exposing environmental problems and helping to find solutions to preserve nature. Since Native Americans have a special bond with nature, they are involved in many of the same activities as Greenpeace. The Mohawk leaders at Akwesasne turned to the organization in the summer of 1988 to draw attention to industry polluting the St.

Lawrence River. Members of Greenpeace sailed up the St. Lawrence and docked at Akwesasne. Four brave members of the crew climbed a water tower and a smokestack and displayed banners that condemned the companies causing the pollution of the river. The local press helped draw attention to Greenpeace's message and the St. Lawrence River was saved.

By 1980, the older population had increased by 100 percent and the younger group had decreased by 50 percent. The Indian Health Service of the federal government, which collects such statistics, offers the following interpretation: "This not only indicates that people are living longer, but that they are moving home after they reach retirement age."[60]

Education

At all age levels, the Mohawk are concerned about the education of their people. In 1979, a group of parents were bothered by the fact that Mohawk children in the local schools were not being taught about their tradition and culture. Some parents decided to create a school of their own in which the parents would make all decisions. As a result, the Akwesasne Freedom School was founded in 1980. The school emphasizes the culture and history of the Mohawk people and their language. In this elementary school, each day begins with the "Thanksgiving Address" recited to Mother Earth in the Mohawk language, and the culture lessons include the cycle of ceremonies that take place during the seasons of the year. About seventy students attend the school. They receive instruction in their native language as well as in the traditional academic subjects of reading, writing, mathematics, science, and history. On the Akwesasne website, the founders of the school explain its purpose: "We would like to help the outside communities understand the cultural and historical significance of the Kaniekeha people and

to reinstate the beliefs and customs that have survived for thousands of years."[61]

In 2001, a day-care service, the first in the state of New York to be licensed by a tribe, opened at Saint Regis. The center came about through a donation from the Alcoa Foundation and General Motors and is part of a neighborhood network-training center for teaching computer and personal development workshops. Authorities from the school told *Indian Country* reporters, "The center is trying to incorporate Native culture into its plans."[62]

In addition to these programs, the Saint Regis Mohawk tribe has sponsored other educational programs for adults, ranging from adult basic education and GED classes to college extension courses through local colleges leading to bachelors and masters degrees. In 2002, sixty-eight students from the reservation enrolled in postsecondary programs. Eight are enrolled in graduate programs. Pride in the educational achievements of these students is recorded on the Indian Health Service Web page: "Twenty-two students graduated from programs receiving certificates in specialized fields. They attended twelve schools in the New York State and three schools in other states."[63]

In a study covering the time period from 1990 to 1991, the New York State Education Department reported that Native American college students, 38 percent of whom were from the Saint Regis Mohawk Reservation, expressed interest in the following employment areas: education, health services, counseling and human services, law, and business and finance. Although some future interests of the college-bound Native Americans lie in the field of human services, other young adults continue to be interested in more traditional Mohawk occupations.

Occupations of the Mohawk

The Mohawk have expanded into new ventures while maintaining some interest in traditional work. Today, as in centuries past, the Mohawk people produce visual works of art. Wall hangings, woven grass baskets, paintings, and jewelry are on display in most cultural center gift shops. Some of these, like the works of Janet Marie Rogers, can be seen at the National Museum of the American Indian in Washington, D.C. Rogers works in various media, including acrylic on deer or cowhide, metal, and beadwork.

Many Mohawk writers tell their stories in poetry and prose. They pass on their heritage through the written word. Janet Marie Rogers has produced two books of poetry: *Facts of Art (Artifacts)* and *Hard (NYC)*. Salli Benedict wrote a poem about her aunt, a basket maker, that describes the woman's closeness to the earth and her ability to stand on a rock, smell the air, and determine where she could look to find sweet grass to weave her baskets.

The Mohawk Touch the Sky

Steelwork is a tradition with the Mohawk. From their Iroquoian roots, the name "Hodinoso:ni" literally means "House Builders." The longhouse of the Iroquois is a structure built piece by piece. Ironwork is constructed in much the same way. Writer Richard Hill, a Native American of the Tuscarora tribe, tells how the two are similar:

> Construction is a Woodland Indian tradition itself. Look at the ancient 'Sky Cities' of the Mound Builders that still stand after several thousand years. Ironworkers perform a very ancient skill—they build structures, not unlike their ancestors who built 200-foot long longhouses. . . . Building is part of our tribal identity.[64]

Hill also makes another interesting comparison between the ironworker of today and traditional Mohawk jobs:

> Ironworkers of today, like the traders and trappers of the past, travel great distances seeking the advantage of the next job, and secure goods for their families back home. For men, Ironwork provides an immediate opportunity to prove yourself, to show your skills and to gain respect of others. Such opportunity allows the men to develop a lot of self-confidence. Ironworkers are providers, a traditional role for men.[65]

National Geographic writer Robert Conly notes that many of the buildings on the New York skyline were constructed with the help of Mohawk workers:

Visitors enter the National Museum of the American Indian in New York to view an exhibit showing Mohawk ironworkers' contributions to the building of New York City.

The first Mohawks I saw were putting up steel for the United Nations' new General Assembly building next to the East River. But even the lofty UN buildings were dwarfed by some other structures I could see against the horizon. Mohawks had helped erect them too: the Metropolitan Life Tower (700 feet tall), the Woolworth Building (792 feet), the RCA Building (850 feet), and, outreaching them all, the Empire State Building which, with its . . . television tower, soars 1,472 feet, more than a quarter of a mile.[66]

Builders recognize that it takes a special type of person to perform well working more than a thousand feet above the ground. H.B. Moyer, who was the director of the National Society for Professional Engineers, describes the characteristics of the Mohawk men that make them suitable for the dangerous construction occupation: "Most possess a cool, clear head, a faculty for meeting and overcoming adverse conditions of all kinds, the knack of thinking in time of emergency, and an endowment of the highest technical skill."[67]

Despite being well suited to the task of constructing skyscrapers, tragedy has claimed the lives of some Mohawk men. In 1907 a span of the Quebec Bridge collapsed during construction. Thirty-three men from Kahnawake were killed. They were buried in the Kahnawake cemetery under crosses made of steel beams. The tragedy, however, did not stop other young men from pursuing the trade.

Today, young Mohawk men and women are still being trained as ironworkers. In Broadview, Illinois, the National Ironworkers Training Program for American Indians instructs youths from across the country. The program graduates about forty new ironworkers each year.

Casinos

Like many other modern-day tribes, the Mohawk have set aside part of their reservation territory and used it to create resort activities to bring money to their people. In fact, as early as 1991, over half the Native American reservations in the United States had some form of gambling. At Akwesasne, the tourists' gambling helps the Mohawk make a living. The Mohawk Bingo Palace and Mohawk Tribal Bingo are two successful New York casinos. Writer Richard Hornung describes the

Workers put the finishing touches on the new Akwesasne Mohawk Casino. At this opening, the casino was one of only two Indian casinos in New York State.

popularity of the casino: "Over a two year span of time, casinos generated millions in cash, overturned the political, economic and social orders: bingo chieftains were the new elite. Money became the new way to measure status—not tracking a deer and shooting a bow."[68] The Mohawk who favor gambling think of it as a valuable enterprise for the tribe because the new wealth makes them independent as a nation.

But not all the Mohawk people are in favor of this newfound way to bring money in to the reservation. The Mohawk Bingo Palace was an overnight success and others are planned. Jake Swamp, an Akwesasne Mohawk chief, speaks out about the abuses: "Gambling will ruin what we still have a chance to hold on to—knowledge of our past and respect for our ancestors."[69]

One man who opposed gambling at Akwesasne did something about it. Tom Porter helped found the Akwesasne Freedom School. He also started Partridge House, a drug and alcohol rehabilitation center. In 1993, Porter, with a group of other like-minded Mohawk, founded Kanatshiohare, "The Clean Pot," in support of the Mohawk spiritual beliefs. There is no gambling, violence, drugs, or alcohol. The group farms organic vegetables, operates a bed and breakfast, has a craft shop, and brings traditional social singing, dancing, and bead/basket-weaving demonstrations to New York City.

The Mohawk's Struggles and Hopes

The problems over land and the authority to govern themselves are much the same for the Mohawk today as they have been over the last centuries. In Akwesasne, because of geographic boundaries, one Mohawk community lives under five external governments: three governing bodies within the reservation and two external agencies, one representative of the United States and the other of Canada. Dealing with layers of authority has often created divisions for people on the reservation and sometimes resulted in unlawful behavior related to smuggling cigarettes, liquor, and drugs.

Although some occupations have changed and new sources of income have replaced traditional jobs, the fundamental character of the Mohawk people has many of the same values as generations ago. For the most part, they have a deep bond with one another and a love of nature. Pollution on the reservation and concern for preserving Mother Earth have led them to become active in Greenpeace, an environmental protection group. The organization aims to heighten citizen awareness of pollution issues and fight corporations that endanger natural resources and bring health problems to the people.

In *Life and Death in Mohawk Country*, writer Bruce Johansen, a professor of communications and Native American studies, sums up the prospects for the Mohawk in the twenty-first century:

"Although Mohawks . . . cannot forget they live in a community still racked by acute turmoil, there is little doubt in their minds that the Mohawks will survive spiritually, culturally, economically, and environmentally. The Great Law of Peace is too much a part of the Mohawks' psyche and soul to be abandoned; the roots of the symbolic Tree of Peace run deep and secure."[70]

In 1994, the state of New York passed legislation to preserve, promote, and celebrate the natural, cultural, and historic treasures of the Mohawk River Valley. It was once the home of thousands of Iroquois Indians. Today, even though much of the land that was once theirs has been taken away, their history remains. Treasures of the Mohawk valley within a 130-by-70-mile area, the Mohawk Valley Heritage Corridor, honor the natural beauty and cultural landmarks of the historic past. Among these, the story of the Iroquois Confederacy has made a lasting mark.

Notes

Chapter 1: The Place of Flint

1. Quoted in Dean R. Snow, Charles T. Gehring, and William A. Starna, eds., *In Mohawk Country*. Syracuse, NY: Syracuse University Press, 1996, p. 39.
2. Quoted in Snow, Gehring, and Starna, *In Mohawk Country*, p. 145.
3. Harmen Meyndertsz van den Bogaert, *A Journey into Mohawk and Oneida Country, 1634–1635*, trans. and ed. Charles T. Gehring and William A. Starna. Syracuse, NY: Syracuse University Press, 1988, p. 3.
4. Van den Bogaert, *A Journey into Mohawk and Oneida Country,* p. 4.
5. Dean R. Snow, *Mohawk Valley Archaeology: The Sites.* University Park: Pennsylvania State University, 1995, p. 164.
6. Dean R. Snow, *The Iroquois.* Cambridge, MA: Blackwell, 1994, p. 127.
7. Quoted in *The Six Nations of New York: The 1892 United States Extra Census Bulletin.* Ithaca, NY: Cornell University Press, 1995, p. vii.
8. Hazel W. Hertzberg, *The Great Tree and the Longhouse.* New York: Macmillan, 1966, p. 97.

Chapter 2: People of the Place of Flint

9. Hertzberg, *The Great Tree and the Longhouse,* p. 27.
10. Lewis Henry Morgan, *The League of the Iroquois.* 1851. Reprint: North Dighton, MA: JG Press, 1995, p. 309.
11. Quoted in Snow, Gehring, and Starna, *In Mohawk Country,* p. 43.
12. Morgan, *The League of the Iroquois*, p. 309.
13. Joseph Bruchac, "A Mohawk Village in 1491: Otstungo," *National Geographic*, October 1991, p. 70.
14. Bruchac, "A Mohawk Village in 1491," p. 78.
15. Hertzberg, *The Great Tree and the Longhouse*, p. 77.
16. Quoted in Snow, Gehring, and Starna, *In Mohawk Country*, p. 42.
17. Bruchac, "A Mohawk Village in 1491," p. 78.
18. Morgan, *The League of the Iroquois*, p. 6.
19. Snow, *The Iroquois*, p. 29.

Chapter 3: The Friends and Enemies of the Mohawk

20. Gehring and Starna, Preface to van den Bogaert, *A Journey into Mohawk and Oneida Country*, p. xiii.
21. Snow, *The Iroquois*, p. 81.

22. Gehring and Starna, Preface to van den Bogaert, *A Journey into Mohawk and Oneida Country*, p. xvii.

23. Quoted in Snow, Gehring, and Starna, *In Mohawk Country*, p. 31.

24. Snow, *The Iroquois*, p. 54.

25. Quoted in Snow, Gehring, and Starna, *In Mohawk Country*, p. 122.

26. Snow, *The Iroquois*, p. 57.

27. Snow, *The Iroquois*, p. 151.

28. Quoted in William W. Campbell, *Annals of Tryon County: Or Border Warfare of New York During the Revolution*. New York: J. & J. Harper, 1831, p. 78.

29. Quoted in New York State Division of Commerce, "Sir William Johnson and Johnson Hall," 2001. www.johnstown.com.

30. Quoted in Campbell, *Annals of Tryon County*, p. 116.

Chapter 4: Ceremonies and Rituals

31. Hertzberg, *The Great Tree and the Longhouse*, p. 4.

32. Hertzberg, *The Great Tree and the Longhouse*, p. 62.

33. Quoted in Snow, Gehring, and Starna, *In Mohawk Country*, p. 120.

34. Quoted in Virgil J. Vogel, *American Indian Medicine*. Norman: University of Oklahoma Press, 1970, p. 49.

35. Quoted in Vogel, *American Indian Medicine*, p. 247.

36. Quoted in Vogel, *American Indian Medicine*, p. 310.

37. Snow, *The Iroquois*, p. 102.

38. Hertzberg, *The Great Tree and the Longhouse*, p. 79.

39. Quoted in William N. Fenton, *The False Faces of the Iroquois*. Norman: University of Oklahoma Press, 1987, p. 76.

40. Van den Bogaert, *A Journey into Mohawk and Oneida Country*, p. 10.

41. Gilbert W. Hagerty, *Wampum, War, and Trade Goods*. Interlaken, NY: Heart of the Lakes Publishing, 1985, p. 51.

42. Morgan, *The League of the Iroquois*, p. 167.

43. Van den Bogaert, *A Journey into Mohawk and Oneida Country*, p. 12.

Chapter 5: Lost Lands and New Lifestyles

44. Peter Nabokov, *Native American Testimony: A Chronicle of Indian-White Relations from Prophecy to the Present, 1492–1992*. New York: Penguin Group, 1991, p. 92.

45. Indian Affairs: Laws and Treaties, "Agreement with the Seneca," 1797. http://digital.library.okstate.edu.

46. Snow, *The Iroquois*, p. 155.

47. Snow, *The Iroquois*, p. 179.

48. David Blanchard, *Seven Generations: A History of the Kaniekehaka*. Quebec, Canada: Kahnawake Survival School, 1980, p. 362.

49. Snow, *The Iroquois*, p. 180.

50. Blanchard, *Seven Generations*, p. 363.

51. Quoted in Blanchard, *Seven Generations*, p. 367.

52. Quoted in Eleanor Burke Leacock and Nancy Oestreich Lurie, eds., *North American Indians in Historical Perspective*. New York: Random House, 1971, p. 161.

53. Quoted in Leacock and Lurie, *North American Indians in Historical Perspective*, p. 150.

54. Blanchard, *Seven Generations*, p. 328.

55. Snow, *The Iroquois*, p. 178.

56. Blanchard, *Seven Generations*, p. 339.

57. Blanchard, *Seven Generations*, p. 344.

58. Blanchard, *Seven Generations*, p. 351.

Chapter 6: The Mohawk in the Twenty-First Century

59. Kanesatake Cultural Centre, "Kanesatake History Brief," 2001. www.schoolnet.ca.

60. Indian Health Service, "Saint Regis Mohawk Tribe of New York—Population," 2001. www.ihs.gov.

61. Akwesasne Freedom School, "History of the Akwesasne Freedom School," 2002. www.potsdam.edu.

62. "Saint Regis Band of Mohawk Indians of New York," *Indian Country*. www.indiancountry.com.

63. Indian Health Service, "Saint Regis Mohawk Tribe of New York—Education."

64. Quoted in Joseph Bruchac, ed., *New Voices from the Longhouse*. Greenfield Center, NY: Greenfield Review Press, 1989, p. 125.

65. Quoted in Bruchac, *New Voices from the Longhouse*, p. 126.

66. Robert L. Conly, "The Mohawks Scrape the Sky," *National Geographic*, July 1952, p. 133.

67. Quoted in Bruchac, *New Voices from the Longhouse*, p. 136.

68. Richard Hornung, *One Nation Under the Gun*. New York: Pantheon Books, 1991, p. 27.

69. Quoted in Hornung, *One Nation Under the Gun*, p. 27.

70. Bruce E. Johansen, *Life and Death in Mohawk Country*. Golden, CO: North American Press, 1993, p. 169.

For Further Reading

Jonathan Bolton and Claire Wilson, *Joseph Brant: Mohawk Chief.* New York: Chelsea House, 1992. An informative biography of Joseph Brant, the Mohawk leader of his people.

Nancy Bonvillain, *The Mohawk.* New York: Chelsea House, 1992. Bonvillain describes the history, culture, and traditions of the Mohawk.

Colin G. Calloway, *Indians of the Northeast.* New York: Facts On File, 1991. Calloway gives a description of past and recent history of the native cultures of the Northeast. He explores topics such as land claims, religious freedom, education, and economic development.

Dennis B. Fradin, *Hiawatha: Messenger of Peace.* New York: Margaret McElderry Books, 1992. Fradin's well-written account tells the story of Hiawatha, the leader who founded the government of the Iroquois Confederacy.

Karen Gravelle, *Growing Up Where the Partridge Drums Its Wings.* New York: Franklin Watts, 1997. An account of the social life and customs of the twentieth-century Mohawk in Quebec and New York.

Janet Hubbard-Brown, *The Mohawk Indians.* New York: Chelsea House, 1993. A discussion for young readers of the history, culture, and daily life of the Mohawk in the colonial era.

Works Consulted

Books

David Blanchard, *Seven Generations: A History of the Kaniekehaka.* Quebec Canada: Kahnawake Survival School, 1980. Mohawk historian David Blanchard gives an authentic history of his people.

Joseph Bruchac, ed., *New Voices from the Longhouse.* Greenfield Center, NY: Greenfield Review Press, 1989. This collection of contemporary fiction and nonfiction works by Native American writers gives insight into the lives of present-day Indians and their thoughts about their heritage.

William W. Campbell, *Annals of Tryon County: Or Border Warfare of New York During the Revolution.* New York: J. & J. Harper, 1831. An account of observations of activity in New York during the time of the Revolutionary War.

Cadwallader Colden, *The History of the Five Indian Nations Depending on the Province of New York in America.* Ithaca, NY: Cornell University Press, 1958. Colden, a colonial scholar and political leader, discusses the religion, manners, customs, laws, and forms of government of the Iroquois five nations from 1727 to 1747.

William N. Fenton, *The False Faces of the Iroquois.* Norman: University of Oklahoma Press, 1987. Scholar William Fenton writes about the religion and mythology of the Iroquois people revealed in ceremonies and rites.

————, *The Great Law and the Longhouse.* Norman: University of Oklahoma Press, 1998. A political history of the six nations of the Iroquois Confederacy.

Gilbert W. Hagerty, *Wampum, War, and Trade Goods.* Interlaken, NY: Heart of the Lakes Publishing, 1985. Hagerty gives an insightful account of the Mohawk's problems in dealing with the white man.

Hazel W. Hertzberg, *The Great Tree and the Longhouse.* New York: Macmillan, 1966. Hertzberg discusses the Iroquois traditions as part of a cultural series prepared for the Anthropology Curriculum Study Project.

Richard Hornung, *One Nation Under the Gun*. New York: Pantheon Books, 1991. Hornung describes occupations of the Mohawk in the twentieth century.

Francis Jennings, *The Ambiguous Iroquois Empire*. New York: Norton, 1984. Jennings's history about the true relationships between the European settlers and the Iroquois presents new perspectives on Native American issues.

Bruce E. Johansen, *Life and Death in Mohawk Country*. Golden, CO: North American Press, 1993. Johansen discusses the civil unrest among the Mohawk people resulting from controls imposed by external governments on their tribal system.

Eleanor Burke Leacock and Nancy Oestreich Lurie, eds., *North American Indians in Historical Perspective*. New York: Random House, 1971. A collection of essays by international scholars that focuses on recent Indian history and the ways Native Americans adapt to new circumstances.

Lewis Henry Morgan, *The League of the Iroquois*. 1851. Reprint: North Dighton, MA: JG Press, 1995. Lewis Morgan, the "Father of Anthropology" and an adopted Seneca, gives vivid details about the political, economic, spiritual, and domestic life of the Iroquois people.

Peter Nabokov, *Native American Testimony: A Chronicle of Indian-White Relations from Prophecy to the Present, 1492–1992*. New York: Penguin Group, 1991. Anthropologist Peter Nabokov presents a five-hundred-year history of Native Americans using documents that recorded the interchange between the Europeans and the Native Americans.

Arthur C. Parker, *The History of the Seneca Indians*. Long Island, NY: Ira J. Friedman, 1926. Scholar, historian, and anthropologist Arthur C. Parker records the history of the Seneca tribe.

The Six Nations of New York: The 1892 United States Extra Census Bulletin. Ithaca, NY: Cornell University Press, 1995. With an explanatory introduction by Robert W. Venables, this document outlines the landholdings and views of the Iroquois population during the last decade of the nineteenth century.

Dean R. Snow, *The Iroquois*. Cambridge, MA: Blackwell, 1994. Snow traces the development of the Iroquois Nation from its beginnings to modern-day life on the reservations.

————, *Mohawk Valley Archaeology: The Sites*. University Park: Pennsylvania State University, 1995. Snow, a historical anthropologist, reports on the results of the excavation of archaeological sites in the Mohawk River Valley.

Dean R. Snow, Charles T. Gehring, and William A. Starna, eds., *In Mohawk Country*. Syracuse, NY: Syracuse University Press, 1996. A collection of early narratives by European missionaries and settlers that gives insights about the Mohawk Indians, the early history of New York, and the social life and customs of the people.

Allen W. Trelease, *Indian Affairs in Colonial New York*. Lincoln: University of Nebraska Press, 1960. Trelease explores the relationship between the tribes of the Iroquois Nation and the European settlers in the state of New York.

Harmen Meyndertsz van den Bogaert, *A Journey into Mohawk and Oneida Country, 1634–1635*. Trans. and ed. Charles T. Gehring and William A. Starna. Syracuse, NY: Syracuse University Press, 1988. Van den Bogaert observes the customs and language of the Mohawk tribe during his trip through their territory.

Virgil J. Vogel, *American Indian Medicine*. Norman: University of Oklahoma Press, 1970. Discusses the healing arts of the American Indian and their use of botany and folklore in the practice of medicine.

Clark Wissler, *Indians of the United States*. New York: Doubleday 1966. A comprehensive history of tribes that inhabited North America.

Periodicals

Jim Adams, "Mohawk Ironworkers See Terroist Plane Pass By," *Indian Country*, September 12, 2001.

Akwesasne Notes, "Greenpeace and Akwesasne," Early Summer 1988.

Harvey Arden, "The Fire That Never Dies," *National Geographic*, September 1957.

Joseph Bruchac, "A Mohawk Village in 1491: Otstungo," *National Geographic*, October 1991.

Robert L. Conly, "The Mohawks Scrape the Sky," *National Geographic*, July 1952.

Melanie Gleaves-Hirsch, "Two Kateri Statues Safely Weather the Storm," *Syracuse Online,* September 14, 1998.

Internet Sources

Akwesasne Freedom School, "History of the Akwesasne Freedom School," 2002. www.potsdam.edu.

Hickok Sports, "Sports History: Lacrosse," 2001. www.hickok sports.com.

Historian Interviews: The Measure of a Man, "Ely Parker." www.pbs.org.

Indian Affairs: Laws and Treaties, "Agreement with the Seneca," 1797. http://digital.library.okstate.edu.

Kahonwes, "Haudenosaunee Time Line," 2001. www.kahonwes.com.

Kanatiyosh, "Iroquois Regalia," 1999. http://tuscaroras.com.

Kanesatake Cultural Centre, "Kanesatake History Brief," 2001. www.schoolnet.ca.

MNCC, "Mohawk Nation Council of Chiefs," 2001. www.slic.com.

New York State Division of Commerce, "Sir William Johnson and Johnson Hall," 2001. www.johnstown.com.

Patrick Weissend, "The Great Survey." www2.pcom.net.

Websites

Avalon Project (www.yale.edu). This website from the Yale Law School provides online copies of famous historical documents.

Indian Country (www.indiancountry.com). An online version of the American Indian news source.

Indian Health Service. (www.ihs.gov). This website produced by the U.S. government is a source of information on Indian health and lifestyle.

Mohawk Nation of Akwesasne (www.peacetree.com). The Six Nation website provides history and news about the Iroquois tribes.

Index

agriculture, 13, 28
Akwesasne (reservation)
  casinos at, 78–79
  education at, 75, 79
  facilities at, 74–75
  governing structures of, 79
  Greenpeace and, 74
  ironworkers of, 73
  location of, 9, 74
  population statistics for, 9, 74–75
  alcoholism, 50–51, 64, 79
Akwesasne Freedom School, 75, 79
Algonquin (tribe), 39–40, 61, 69
American Revolution, 40–43, 45
Anglican Church. *See* Church of England
animals, 10–11, 30
Annals of Tryon County (Campbell), 42
anthropology, 23
archaeology, 13–14, 31–32, 54

Bagot Commission, 61
Barentsz, Pieter, 34
basketry, 31
Bear clan, 14
beaver, 9, 33
Benedict, Salli, 76
Big Tree, The Treaty of 58–60
birth control, 27–28
Blanchard, David, 61–62, 65–66, 68
Bogaert, Harmen van den, 12–13, 33, 54, 56
bow and arrow, 38

Brant, Joseph, 41–42, 43, 45
bridge building, 55–67
Bruchac, Joseph, 15, 25, 28, 30
burden litter, 26
burden strap, 26
Bureau of Indian Affairs, 58, 70

Campbell, William W., 42
Canada, 42, 54, 61–62, 64–67
  see also names of reservations
Canassatego (Iroquois leader), 67
cannibalism, 17–18, 19
canoes, 30
casinos, 78–79
Catholic religion, 35, 61, 74
  see also French
Caughnawaga (tribe), 61
Cayuga (tribe), 8, 10, 41, 61
ceremonies, 46–56
Champlain, Samuel de, 39–40
Cherry Valley (battle), 42
chiefs, 21
childbirth, 25–26
children, 25–27
Church of England, 71
clan system, 14–16
climate, 11–12
Clinton, James, 57–58
Colden, Cadwallader, 52
colonists, 9, 14, 33–37
Confederacy Chief, 21
Conly, Robert, 76–77

Corn Mother, 49
cradle board, 26
cranberry farming, 70–71
creation myth, 12, 15, 19
Crieckenbeeck, Daniel van, 34

Dawes General Allotment Act, 61
death rituals, 54–57
Deganawida (Iroquois "Peacemaker"), 18
diseases, 14, 41, 60
Donck, Adriaen van der, 51–52
Dutch, 9, 20, 33–35

eating, 23
entertainment business, 67–68
environmental protection, 79
    see also Greenpeace; Kahnawake
epidemics, 14, 41, 60
Episcopal Church. See Church of England
Europeans. See colonists
Evil Spirit, 46

face paint, 28
    see also ceremonies; warfare
farming, 13, 28
Fenton, William, 64–65
festivals, 47, 49–50
food, 23–24, 28
Franklin, Benjamin, 67
French, 33, 35, 39–40, 61
fur trade, 33

Garoga (Mohawk village), 13–14, 15–16
    see also archaeology
Gehring, Charles, 33, 34
geography, 10
government, 17–21
Grant, Ulysses S., 63

graves, 55–56
Great Spirit, 45, 46, 47
Great Tree and the Longhouse, The
    (Hertzberg), 21, 22, 28, 46, 49–50
Green Corn Festival, 49
Greenpeace, 74, 79

Hagerty, Gilbert, 54
Handsome Lake, 50–51, 63
Harvest Festival, 49
Hertzberg, Hazel, 21, 22, 28, 46, 49–50,
    53
Hiawatha (Iroquois leader), 17, 18
Hill, Richard, 76
Holland Land Company, 58, 59–60
    see also land ownership
Hornung, Richard, 78–79
Hudson, Henry, 33
    see also Dutch
hunting, 30

In Mohawk Country (Snow), 20, 51
ironworkers, 73
Iroquois, The (Snow), 19, 34, 36–37, 41,
    48, 53, 59, 65
Iroquois Confederacy
    colonial unity and, 67
    destruction of, 61, 156
    formation of, 17–19
    founders of, 18–19
    Franklin and, 67
    government of, 21
    intertribal communication in, 32
    organization of, 20–21
    origins of, 10
    symbols of, 18–19
    tribes of, 8, 10
Iroquois Nation. See Iroquois
    Confederacy

Jogues, Father Isaac, 35
  see also Catholic religion; French
Johansen, Bruce, 79
Johnson, Sir William, 41–42, 43

Kahnawake (reservation)
  bridge builders of, 65–66
  education at, 73–74
  entertainment business and, 67–68
  ironworkers of, 78
  land problems at, 72–73
  police force of, 73
  political rights and, 62, 64
  river pilots of, 65
  United Nations and, 72
Kalm, Peter, 52–53
Kanesatake (reservation), 69–70

lacrosse, 29
Lafitau, Joseph-François, 53, 54
land ownership, 57–61, 64–65
  see also reservations
Le Mercie, François-Joseph, 11
League of the Iroquois. See Iroquois
  Confederacy
League of the Iroquois, The (Morgan), 23,
  25, 35, 55
Life and Death in Mohawk Country
  (Johansen), 79
longhouses
  construction of, 13
  description of, 13, 14
  destruction of community of, 64–65
  furniture in, 24–25
  interior features of, 22–23, 25
  location of, 12, 15–16, 22
  significance of, 9, 12, 18

marriage, 27
matrilineal society, 14–15, 21
medicine bundle, 48
medicine men, 48, 53–54
Megapolensis, Johannes, 10–11, 20,
  23–24, 28
  see also Dutch
Midwinter Festival, 49
migration, 13
Mohawk
  American Revolution and, 40–43, 45
  area inhabited by, 10
  art of, 30–32, 76
  British and, 40, 45
  Canada and, 61–62, 64–65
  canoes of, 30
  carrying devices of, 26
  Catholic religion and, 61
  ceremonies of, 46–56
  Christianity and, 50, 61, 71, 74
  citizenship of, 62, 64
  Civil War and, 65
  clan system of, 14–16
  construction work and, 65–67
  craftsmanship of, 30–32, 76
  customs of, 14–15, 21, 25–28, 55–56
  description of, 28
  diet of, 23–24
  disease and, 35
  Dutch and, 33–35
  education and, 75–76
  entertainment business and, 67–68
  environment of, 10, 20
  farming and, 13
  food of, 23–24
  French and, 40, 45, 61
  Greenpeace and, 79
  hunting and, 30

intertribal communication of, 32
lands of, 10, 20
life expectancy of, 54
medicine and, 35, 51–53
men's role among, 30
migration patterns of, 13
military service and, 65
missionaries and, 35, 50, 61, 71
modern life of, 69–80
names for, 8, 12, 18, 21
naming of individuals and, 49–50
nature and, 30, 46–50, 79
occupations of, 73, 76
police force of, 73
religion of, 12, 15, 30, 46–50
relocation of, 42, 45
reservations of, 69
rivers and, 65
settlements of, 12–13
skyscrapers and, 73, 76–78
sports of, 29
survival of, 45
territory of, 8, 10, 20
tools of, 30
trading and, 30, 33
tribal enemies of, 39–40
United Nations and, 72
unity and, 64–65
values of, 79–80
warfare of, 35–38
weapons of, 30, 36, 38
women's role among, 27–28, 30
Mohawk Nation Council of Chiefs, 69
Mohawk Pledge, 71
Mohawk Valley Archaelogy: The Sites
   (Snow), 15–16
Mohawk Valley Heritage Corridor, 80
Mohawk Village in 1491: Otsungo, A
   (Bruchac), 15, 25, 30

moieties, 16, 54
Morgan, Lewis Henry, 23, 25, 31, 55, 60,
   63
Morris, Robert, 58
Moyer, H.B., 77
Museum of the American Indian, 76
myths, 12, 53–54

Nabokov, Peter, 58
National Geographic (magazine), 76–77
National Ironworkers Training Program
   for American Indians, 78
natural resources, 10–11
nature, 46
New Netherlands, 33–34
Nipissing (tribe), 61, 69

Oka, Quebec, 69–70
   see also Canada; Kanesatake; land own-
      ership
Oneida (tribe), 8, 10, 41
Onondaga (tribe)
   American Revolution and, 41
   Hiawatha and, 18
   Iroquois Confederacy and, 8, 10
   name for, 18
   Six Nations Confederacy and, 61–62
   territory of, 18
oral history, 8, 15
organic farming, 79
Owasco (Mohawk village), 32
   see also archaeology

Parker, Eli, 63
Partridge House, 79
Peacemaker, 18–19
plant life, 10–11
political organization, 17–21

population control, 27–28
Porter, Tom, 79
pottery, 31–32
prayers, 46, 47

Quakers, 50

reservations, 59, 61
Revolutionary War. See American
  Revolution
rituals, 46–56
river pilots, 65
Rogers, Janet Marie, 76

Saint Regis. *See* Akwesasne
saunas, 51, 52
Seneca (tribe)
  American Revolution and, 41
  Iroquois confederacy and, 8, 10
  land ownership and, 58–60
  Parker and, 63
  territory of, 18
settlements. *See* longhouses
Seven Generations (Blanchard), 61–62,
  65–66
shamans, 51
Six Nations Confederacy, 61–62, 64
Six Nations Reserve, 45
smallpox, 14, 35, 60
Snow, Dean, 15–16, 19, 34, 36–37, 41,
  48, 51, 53, 59, 62, 65
snowshoes, 25
sports, 29

St. Lawrence Seaway project, 72
  see also bridge building; Canada; land
  ownership
Starna, William, 33, 34
steelworkers. *See* ironworkers
Swamp, Jake, 79
symbols, 18–19

Tekakwitha, Kateri, 35, 44, 74–75
Thayendenaga. See Brant, Joseph
tomahawk, 38
torture, 14, 17–18
  see also warfare
trading, 30
Treaty of Big Tree, 58–60
Turtle clan, 14, 15
Tuscarora (tribe), 8, 18, 41
Tyendinaga (reservation), 69, 71–72

voyagers, 65

Wahta (reservation), 70–71
wampum, 17, 46
war club, 38
warfare, 35–38
Washington, George, 58
weapons, 30, 36, 38
West India Trade Company, 33–34
wildlife, 30
Wolf clan, 14
women, 27–28, 30
  see also matrilineal society

Picture Credits

© Cover photo: Ted Spiegel/CORBIS

Associated Press, 73

Associated Press, AP/Paul Hawthorne, 77

Associated Press, AP/Michael Okoniewski, 78

© Nathan Benn/CORBIS, 55

© Bettmann/CORBIS, 29

© CORBIS, 52, 59

© Richard Cummins/CORBIS, 44

Hulton Archive by Getty Images, 17, 20, 34, 39, 40, 63, 64, 66

Library of Congress Inc., 43, 60

© Christopher J. Morris/CORBIS, 70

© David Muench/CORBIS, 11

Mary Evans Picture Library, 24, 47, 56

North Wind Picture Archives, 16, 37

© Ted Spiegel/CORBIS, 72

Stock Montage Inc., 23

© Werner Forman Archive/Art Resource, NY, 31, 38, 48

© Marilyn "Angel" Wynn/Nativestock, 12

About the Author

Mary R. Dunn, a native of Ohio, has written both fiction and non-fiction pieces for a children's magazine and articles for education publications. As a literacy specialist, she has taught reading/writing skills in elementary school and at the college level. Currently, she lives in Illinois and enjoys teaching, traveling, reading, and writing.